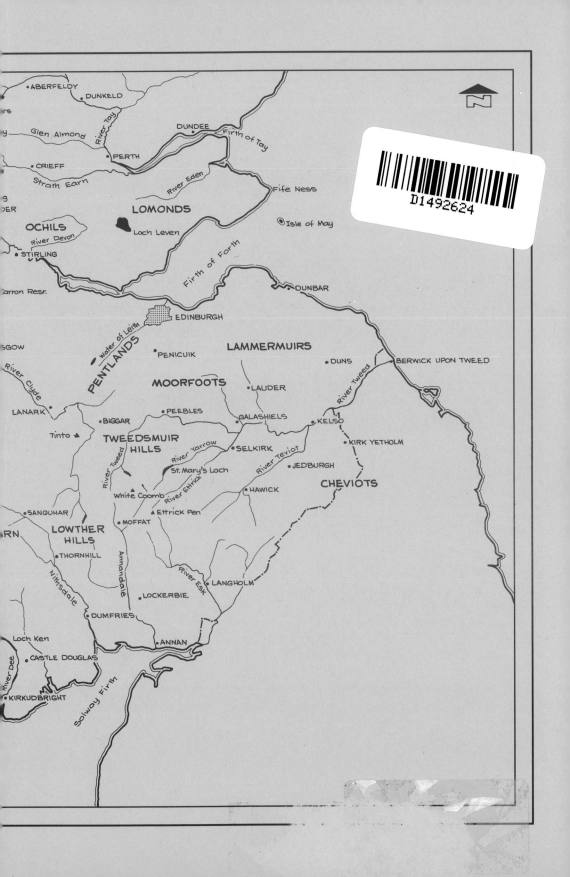

SKI MOUNTAINEERING IN SCOTLAND

SCOTTISH MOUNTAINEERING CLUB
GUIDE
Edited by
DONALD BENNET and BILL WALLACE

First published in Great Britain in 1987 by the Scottish Mountaineering Trust

Copyright © by the Scottish Mountaineering Trust

Ski mountaineering in Scotland.—— (Scottish Mountaineering Club guide).
    1. Mountaineering   2. Skis and skiing
    I. Bennet, Donald J.   II. Wallace, Bill,
    1930 -   III. Series
    796.5'22   GV200

    ISBN 0-907521-20-7

Front Cover: The ascent to Carn Dearg in the Monadh Liath
                  Photo: D.J. Bennet

Rear Cover: Early morning in the Grey Corries
                  Photo: D. Scott

Design by Donald Bennet
Maps drawn by Jim Renny
Production by Peter Hodgkiss
Typesetting by Newtext Composition, Glasgow
Colour separations by Arneg, Glasgow
Printed by Thomson Colour Printers, Glasgow
Bound by Hunter and Foulis, Edinburgh

Distributed by Cordee, 3a DeMontfort Street, Leicester LE1 7HD.

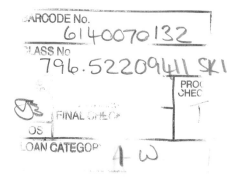

CONTENTS

INTRODUCTION

It is now over sixty years since the publication of the first of the Scottish Mountaineering Club's guidebooks (as distinct from the publication of guidebook articles in SMC Journal). In this time the range and numbers of these books have steadily increased to reflect the widening range of activities and interests of climbers, and their greatly increased skills and improved techniques. The publication of this guide to ski-mountaineering in Scotland is one more step in the extension of this range of books.

This publication is a significant step, for it is the first SMC guidebook to recognise the present status of ski-mountaineering in Scotland. In the past this status has been somewhat undermined by the feeling among some mountaineers in Scotland that the use of skis in mountaineering is not quite a respectable part of their sport, possibly being associated in their minds with the less demanding pleasures of downhill skiing. However, ski-mountaineering has long been established, possibly rather tenuously, as a very respectable part of our sport, enthusiastically pursued by some eminent Scottish mountaineers in the past hundred years. It is appropriate to mention, very briefly, a few of the personalities and events of the early years of ski-mountaineering in Scotland.

In 1892 W.W. Naismith, generally regarded as the founder of the Scottish Mountaineering Club, is reported to have used long wooden planks as skis on the Campsie Hills and he described his experiences with enthusiasm to fellow members of the Club. J.H. Wigner was another early enthusiast who made a ski ascent of Ben Chonzie in 1904, and at the Easter Meet that year W.R. Rickmers endeavoured to teach some members of the Club to ski on Ben Nevis, but his efforts were rather thwarted by continuous rain, a problem which modern ski-mountaineers will readily recognise. After the meet Rickmers presented eleven pairs of skis to the Club, but none have apparently survived to the present day, unlike at least one celebrated ice-axe of the same period. Harold Raeburn, the owner of that axe, was also a skier, but not an enthusiastic one, possibly because his efforts were largely confined to the Pentlands and other low hills, and he saw little prospect of using skis on the higher mountains. He caused consternation one night in Edinburgh by skiing down the tramway lines to Morningside Station on his way home from an expedition to the Pentlands.

The Scottish Ski Club was formed in 1907, and it and the SMC had many members in common. At the SMC's Easter Meet in 1909 Naismith and Allan Arthur carried their skis up Ben Nevis from the Carn Mor Dearg Arête, and then ran and crashed their way down the slopes of the Red Burn. Naismith's enthusiasm for this activity prompted him to write in the same year, addressing his fellow members of the SMC who like their modern counterparts looked askance at ski-mountaineering:

"Will the younger members who have not yet tried skiing allow an old fogey to urge them to take up a sport which bids fair to become a formidable rival of the axe and rope during winter months."

It seems that at the time there was, as there still is, some divergence of opinion between the merits of Alpine and Norwegian skis and bindings, and the techniques best suited to these two types of equipment. Rickmers had been brought up in the Alpine school, and the skis which he presented to the Club were the Lillienfeldt model, designed by Zdarsky and were the forerunner of modern Alpine skis — short, rigid and heavy. Raeburn, on the other hand, favoured the longer, lighter Norwegian skis which were suited for travel over the level and gently undulating

An early party of Scottish ski mountaineers on the south ridge of Stob Binnein   H. MacRobert

country which is characteristic of Scandinavia, and this may explain why he was not enthusiastic about using them on steep hills. Nevertheless he seems to have found them quite suitable for skiing along tramway lines, just as many Nordic skiers nowadays prefer to ski along prepared tracks.

From about 1910 onwards two men emerged as the founders of ski-mountaineering in Scotland as it is now known — Allan Arthur and Harry MacRobert. Their articles in the SMC Journal indicate the enthusiasm of these and other pioneers of this sport, and the widening range of hills that were being climbed and traversed on skis. At the SMC's Easter Meet in Aviemore in 1913 parties crossed the Cairngorms from Glenmore Lodge to Derry Lodge and returned over the Glen Feshie hills. Many of the active ski-mountaineers in the Club were also members of the Scottish Ski Club, thus forming a bond between these two clubs which has grown over the years. In 1932 the Scottish Ski Club built a small hut in Coire Odhar below Beinn Ghlas, one of the Lawers peaks. This hut became a focal point for skiers for the next thirty years, until gradually the development of skiing centres elsewhere in Scotland from 1956 onwards drew skiers away from the simple pleasures of Ben Lawers to the ski-tows and chair-lifts of Cairn Gorm, Glen Shee and Meall a' Bhuiridh.

One ski-mountaineer whose activities in Scotland spanned the years before and after the Second World War was Willie Speirs. He imported his first pair of skis from Switzerland in 1928, learned to ski on the Campsies and was still active forty years later. His expeditions in Scotland between 1928 and 1965 included Meall a' Bhuiridh in 1932, possibly the first ski descent of the mountain which twenty five years later was a focal point in the development of mass downhill skiing in Scotland. That must have been a great descent down the north-east corrie of the mountain with not another person or a pylon in sight.

The years since the war have seen growing numbers of mountaineers turned skiers, and skiers turned mountaineers, but for twenty years the growth in the sport seemed to be unspectacular. Its proponents were not given to publish their achievements and enthusiasms widely, and the mountaineers among them have been inhibited by the feeling that prevailed among their 'hard' fellow-mountaineers that the development of downhill skiing in Scotland was something with which no true mountaineer should have any dealings.

The first traverse of the four Cairngorm 4000-ft mountains in 1953 by Norman Clark was a landmark, and in the north-east the Adam Watsons, father and son, were active skiers over all the hills of Deeside from the low tops of Bennachie and Clachnaben to the high Cairngorms. The younger Adam's traverse of Ben Avon and the five highest Cairngorms in 1962 was an outstanding feat, and an eloquent demonstration of the potential of Nordic skis in the Cairngorms, given the right conditions.

The standard of ski-mountaineering was also improving, aided no doubt by the developing downhill facilities in Scotland, and the increasing numbers of skiers going to the Alps for both downhill and mountain skiing. No one exemplified these standards better than John Wilson whose style, skill and unerring route finding ability were an example to those who followed him up the ridges and down the corries of Ben Lawers, often in conditions of storm and white-out, at touring meets of the Scottish Ski Club.

The publication by Malcolm Slesser in 1970 of his book *Scottish Mountains on Ski* was a revelation of the great range of ski-mountaineering possibilities in Scotland, and this book stimulated a lot of interest. Slesser was among

The Scottish Ski Club hut in Coire Odhar, Ben Lawers   *H.M. Brown*

the first to attempt the Scottish High Level Route, the traverse on skis from the Deeside hills to Ben Nevis (or vice-versa). This long and demanding expedition requires a week of good weather and good snow cover, neither of which is likely in Scotland, and adverse conditions foiled many attempts until the traverse from Ben Avon to Ben Nevis was accomplished in March 1978 by Mike Taylor and David Grieve.

Now the role which ski-mountaineering plays in the wider sport is well established, not only in Scotland, but to a much greater extent elsewhere. One has only to look at the journals of the European alpine clubs, and books and magazines on alpine climbing, to realise that in the Alps in winter, spring and early summer ski-mountaineering is the predominant activity, making it possible to climb and traverse the high mountains in those seasons when on foot it would be impossible. In Scotland the role of ski-mountaineering is less important because it is not necessary, unless in exceptional conditions of very deep soft snow, to use skis to climb in winter. It may be more pleasant, but it is seldom essential.

Those who have become addicted to ski-mountaineering in Scotland would claim that this combination of skiing and winter mountain walking brings added interest, enjoyment and excitment to both sports. As Sandy Wedderburn, another highly talented SMC climber and skier put it in his book *Alpine Climbing on Foot and with Ski,* it is a sport which "has added a new and most delectable pleasure to mountain going." Greater interest and importance is attached to correct route selection and the discovery of new, untracked and possibly challenging downhill runs gives the skier far more excitement than he is likely to find on the beaten piste. There are conditions, such as deep soft snow, when the skier will find it much easier than the walker to reach the summits, but it would be wrong in general to claim that the ascent is easier and faster for the skier than the walker, it all depends on the snow conditions. Going downhill, of course, the situation is quite different and the skier should not only be much faster, but will have the added pleasure of the downhill run, that joy of smooth motion and thrill of speed. The only disadvantage is that this pleasure is all too brief, and before long skins have to be put back on skis for the next uphill climb.

It is not the intention that this guide should be a textbook of ski-mountaineering. One such book is being published at the same time as this guide, *Ski Mountaineering* by Peter Cliff, published by Unwin Hyman (1987), and it contains all the necessary technical information on all aspects of ski-mountaineering. However, some brief remarks about Scottish mountain conditions and the use of this guide are necessary.

Two factors which determine the character of any Scottish mountain climb in winter are snow and weather conditions, and they influence a ski-mountaineering day as much if not more than a day walking or climbing on snow and ice. In this context it must be stressed that the illustrations in this guide are not representative of typical Scottish conditions; the sun does not shine all the time, nor are the mountains always white!

Snow conditions are such an important factor in a day's ski-mountaineering that they should be considered carefully before setting out. The variation of snow type — ice, nevé, crusted snow, spring snow, powder snow, windslab and porridge to name some — has a great bearing on the pleasure and safety of the day. These conditions can vary according to the orientation of the mountainside one is planning to ascend and descend, and conditions on opposite sides of a mountain on any day can be very different. One should take into account not only the

Looking south-west from Stob Coire Easain in the Grey Corries   *C.R. Ford*

weather on the day itself, but also the weather during the preceding week, in particular the amount of snow or rainfall, the wind strength and direction and temperature changes. With these in mind it should be possible to predict snow conditions and chose a mountain and a route that will give good and safe skiing. For example, strong winds during and soon after snowfall can leave the windward side of a mountain and its exposed ridges blown clear of snow, while leeward sides may have big accumulations. Warm south-west winds will soon strip the snow off slopes facing in that direction, while cycles of freezing and thawing will produce hard snow or ice which may make even gentle slopes potentially dangerous.

Avalanche conditions are likely to exist in the days following heavy snowfall until the fresh snow has consolidated, and the effect of wind on the surface of newly fallen snow to produce the crust called windslab is particularly dangerous. For a much more detailed treatment of the avalanche hazard readers are referred to *A Chance in a Million. Scottish Avalanches,* by Bob Barton and Blyth Wright, published by the Scottish Mountaineering Trust (1985).

Bad weather brings with it all the problems of mountain navigation which are familiar to all mountaineers, but may not be so familiar to downhill skiers who rely on piste markers for guidance. The ski-mountaineer has additional problems to overcome, for whereas the hillwalker can in bad visibility take a bearing and walk on it with little or no deviation (provided he is careful), the skier will often find it harder or even impossible to ski on a bearing as steep slopes, minor crags and patches of bare scree and rock will force detours from the correct bearing. The effects of such detours have to be allowed for. Problems of navigation when going uphill are small compared to those when descending, for skiing downhill in a straight line on a bearing is no easy matter except on very easy angled terrain. If one is skiing steeply downhill on a zig-zag course accurate navigation becomes very difficult. One may have to take off skis and walk, or keep skins on to reduce the downhill speed and thus ski straight down a slope that would otherwise require turns. It is also very difficult to judge distances travelled when skiing in bad visibility, particularly when making repeated turns.

To summarise, ski mountaineers must recognise that their sport is potentially more dangerous than either downhill skiing or hill walking, and they should take precautions accordingly. The hazards of skiing downhill from a mountain top on an unknown route in zero visibility are considerable, particularly if there are crags and cornices anywhere near at hand. There are bound to be times when the sensible course of action is to take off skis and walk, no matter how frustrating this may be.

The accurate use of the map and compass is of course essential, and the present Ordnance Survey 1:50000 Second Series and Landranger Series maps are the standard mountaineers' maps in this country. A compass mounted on a wrist strap outside the sleeve of one's anorak is particularly useful when both one's hands are involved with ski poles. The use of an aneriod altimeter is a useful aid to navigation provided it is sufficiently accurate. Such an instrument should be capable of showing changes of height of 10 metres, and is thus very useful in fixing one's position by relating to contour lines on the map, provided it has been correctly set before starting out from the foot of the hill. It should be remembered that in high winds there are local pressure variations on mountain summits which cause the aneroid to overestimate the height due to locally high winds. Thus, in a high wind one may reach a summit which the map shows as 1000m and find that the aneroid reads slightly higher, e.g. 1030m.

Gradients of slopes can be calculated from the map by measuring the distance between contour lines. As an example, if the distance measured on the OS 1:50000 Second Series map between two adjacent thick contour lines (representing a vertical height difference of 50m) is 2mm, the slope can be calculated by those familiar with trigonometry as 27°, which may give the impression that it is not very steep. It is in fact quite steep for the skier, as steep as the upper part of the Tiger Run on The Cairnwell in Glen Shee. The following table gives gradients and the very approximate relationship between them and the difficulty ratings used in this guide.

Distance between adjacent thick contour lines	Angle of slope	Approximate equivalent rating of difficulty
2mm	27°	IV
3mm	18½°	III
4mm	14°	III
5mm	11½°	II
6mm	9½°	II
8mm	7°	I
10mm	5½°	I

For comparison purposes, the gradients (average) of some well known ski runs in Scotland are given.

Tiger Run, The Cairnwell	27°
White Lady, Cairn Gorm	20°
Main Run, Meall a' Bhuiridh	18°
Coire Cas, Cairn Gorm	13°
Fiacaill Run, Cairn Gorm	15°

As regards equipment for ski-mountaineering, it is not the intention of this guide to enter the controversy between Alpine and Nordic equipment that dates back to the days of Naismith and Raeburn. However, it is generally considered that Alpine equipment is more suited than Nordic equipment for the majority of the ski-mountaneering tours described in this book. There is no doubt that in favourable conditions many of these tours could be undertaken with Nordic skis, but on the whole Alpine skis are preferable when it comes to skiing in the difficult and unpreditable conditions that are all too common in Scotland.

The three main items of equipment are of course skis, preferably light and designed for mountaineering, bindings designed for touring with full heel lift and normal safety features, and ski-mountaineering boots which are considerably lighter and more comfortable than downhill-only boots for walking. Skins are essential for climbing anything but the easiest of slopes, and the 'stick-on' variety are now the most popular, preferably with front and rear fixings for extra security in the event of the glue losing its adhesion. Harscheisen (ski crampons) are essential for climbing steep and icy slopes, although they are not needed in soft snow. Ice axe and crampons should also be taken on tours over steep mountains where it may possibly be necessary to take off skis and climb on foot, and a rucksack with suitable straps for attaching skis when they have to be carried is advantageous. On easy tours ice axe and crampons may not be necessary, but any decision not to take them should only be made with due consideration.

For tours in the Cairngorms and the remote mountains of the north and north-west, where parties must be totally self-sufficient, survival gear should be taken, including spare clothing, adequate food, first aid kit and possibly also a sleeping bag and snow shovel for a possible overnight emergency.

The routes described in this guide are for the most part the logical ski routes in normal winter conditions. Obviously abnormal snow conditions may force parties to choose alternative routes, and invariably the ski mountaineer has to make route finding decisions based on the snow conditions and snow cover that he encounters. The distances quoted are for the complete tour from start to finish. The height climbed is the total height, including any intermediate tops and reascents in the course of a traverse. The time given is based on the judgement of the author, and is the time that should be taken by a reasonably fit party in average conditions without any long stops. The maps indicate the routes by red lines, with alternative routes shown by dashed lines.

In the text the distinction is made between heights climbed and distances travelled horizontally, both of which may be given in metres, by using the abbreviation m for metres (e.g. 150m) when referring to heights, and spelling metres in full when referring to distances.

The rating system is an attempt on the part of the authors and editors to convey the quality and difficulty of the tours described. The quality, character and ambience of a tour is indicated by a scale which may be interpreted approximately as follows:-

★★ = modest;   ★★★ = good;   ★★★★ = very good;   ★★★★★ = excellent.
(One star tours are not of sufficient quality to be included in this book).

The technical difficulty of a tour, which refers to its most difficult passage and not its average difficulty, may be equated to the difficulty of alpine pistes approximately as follows:-

II = a blue run;   III = a red run;   IV = a black run.

It is however, recognised that these ratings are approximate and subjective, and readers may prefer to ignore them and form their own opinions. It is far more important that ski-mountaineers should develop their own judgement based on experience. Only then will they enjoy the freedom of the hills and the pleasure of skiing over them.

On the Campsie Fells at dusk   *D.J. Bennet*

The Campsie Fells are the nearest hills to Glasgow with any potential for skiing, although their character of extensive plateau-like tops surrounded by steep slopes and escarpments makes them more suitable for cross-country than downhill skiing. The nature of the terrain of these tops, tussocky grass and eroded peat banks, makes a good cover of snow essential for skiing, but such snow cover is rather rare for the Campsies reach only 578m at their highest. However, when the conditions are right, there are some good short tours that are well worth doing.

The easiest and highest access is from the B822 road from Lennoxtown to Fintry which crosses the Campsies and reaches a height of 330m. From the top of this road one can make tours to the E and W. Eastwards there is a circular traverse over Lairs, Cort-ma Law and Lecket Hill, which can be extended to Meikle Bin, but recent forestry plantings have made access to this hill more difficult. Westwards one can traverse Hole Head and Hart Hill across an extensive and featureless plateau, and possibly get some downhill running with a descent S to Clachan of Campsie.

Earl's Seat, the highest of the Campsies, can be reached from the S either up the long ridge on the SW side of the Fin Glen over Dumbreck, or from Blanefield, starting up the 'pipe road' and traversing NW below the long escarpment of Slackdhu to reach easier slopes leading to Clachertyfarlie Knowes and Earl's Seat.

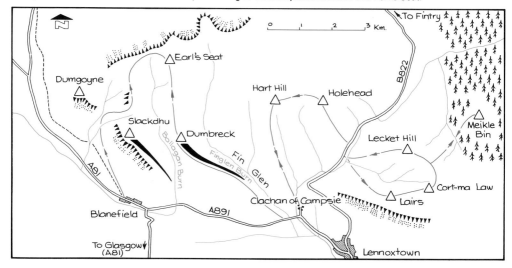

The ridge between Turnhouse Hill (left) and the Kips (right) W. Wallace

The Traverse from Nine Mile Burn (177577) to Hillend (250670).
Distance 13 km. Height climbed 650 m. Time 4-5 hours.

This traverse is a fine tour but, due to the relatively low elevation of the hills, snow seldom accumulates in sufficient quantity to make a ski traverse possible. Nevertheless, the terrain is grass covered which permits skiing on minimal snow cover.

To complete the whole traverse it is necessary to have transport from Hillend at the Edinburgh city boundary on the A702 road to Nine Mile Burn (there is an infrequent bus service). However, any of the hills may be ascended singly or in groups from the A702.

From Nine Mile Burn ascend N up an easy slope to reach the final steep rise to the West Kip. Continue NE over the East Kip, then descend to the col beyond. Make a rising traverse across the NW slope of Scald Law, the highest top, to the summit. From there the route continues NE over Carnethy Hill to Turnhouse Hill, then descends E past a few wind-blown trees to a footbridge across the Glencorse Burn to join the road to Glencorse Reservoir.

If there is no firing taking place on Castlelaw range, go up the road towards the reservoir to a gate on the right then ascend NE to join the track which passes round the E side of Castlelaw Hill. (An alternative route to avoid the firing range goes round the W side of the hill starting from the N corner of the reservoir). Continue N to Allermuir then turn E and pass over Caerketton, continuing along the ridge until E of the chairlift where easy slopes lead down to the A702 road at Hillend.

Two short tours, suitable for a morning or afternoon, are the traverse of Allermuir and Caerketton from Swanston village (240673), and the traverse of Capelaw Hill and Allermuir from Bonaly (214679).

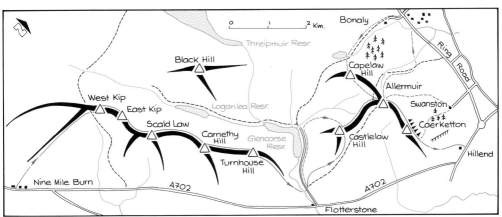

Tinto from Culter Fell   *D.J. Bennet*

Tinto; 707m; (OS Sheet 72; 953343).
Starting points: There are several possible starting places on the roads round Tinto; altitude about 250m. Distances 6-8km. Height climbed 330-460m. Time 2-4 hours. Rating: ★★/III.

Tinto is the most prominent hill in the upper Clyde valley, set among open rolling country which is very different from the Highland landscape. Being less than an hour's drive from Edinburgh or Glasgow, it is very accessible and is encircled by roads; the A83, B7075, and minor roads by Fallburn, Woodend, Lochlyoch and Howgate farms. Thus it is a very good hill for a short day out, an afternoon or even an evening sortie. I have on one occasion in late February left Glasgow after work, skied up the north side of Tinto to arrive at the summit after sunset and returned to the road by torchlight across smooth snowfields reflecting the last of the alpenglow.

The choice of the best ski route up Tinto is always dependant on conditions such as the wind direction during

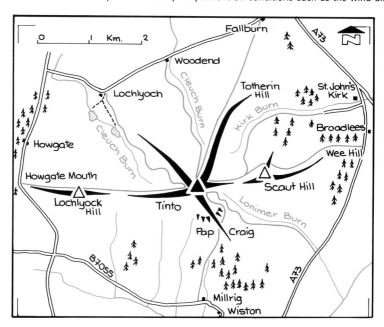

recent snowfalls. It may be worth circling the hill to assess the best snow cover. Streams, shelter belts of trees, walls and fences can often create ribbons of snow when other parts of the hill are bare.

The map opposite shows possible routes on all sides of the hill. If your party has two cars, it may be possible to do an interesting traverse, otherwise the descent route is likely to be near the ascent.

On the north side, the road between Fallburn and Lochlyoch farms gives easy access to the fields beyond which one reaches the steeper rounded NW shoulder of Tinto between the two Cleuch burns. Further east the route starting from the car park near Fallburn, up the shoulder of Totherin Hill and along the fence to the summit gives good views across the northern slopes of Tinto.

On the west the summit of the road at Howgate Mouth is the highest starting point (c.380m), and the route goes along the ridge over Lochlyock Hill. This is a good way if there is a fresh west wind blowing.

On the south one can start at Millrig and climb N towards the steep scar of Pap Craig, which must be avoided. This is the shortest and steepest ascent. A good descent can be made SE from the summit steeply down into the high corrie of the Lanimer Burn, ending across moorland and fields.

To the east of Tinto one can start near Broadlees and go up on the S side of the plantation to Wee Hill, and continue SW along the ridge following a track over Scaut Hill and along a fence to the summit. The descent can be varied by skiing down the Kirk Burn to St. John's Kirk.

Culter Fell; 748m; (OS Sheet 72; 053291).

Starting points: There are several around the hill, the nearest one being at (032305) ½km south of Birthwood in the valley of the Culter Water 3½km south of Coulter. From there: Distance 6km. Height climbed 490m. Time 2-3 hours. Rating: ★★/III.

Unlike Tinto, which is very much an isolated hill, Culter Fell is surrounded by lower tops. It is the highest point of a large area of many grassy rounded hills between the valleys of the Clyde and the Tweed rivers. From the main roads in these two valleys several minor roads lead up the higher valleys towards Culter Fell itself.

The shortest ascent, one that can easily be done in a short winter's afternoon, starts from the Culter Water. From Coulter village on the A702 road take the narrow road up the Culter Water to a point ½km beyond Birthwood, at the foot of Kings Beck. Climb the heathery ridge of Shin Fell, following a track at first, to the summit. Ski N along a fence for ½km to a flat col, and then NE down the ridge on the N side of Kings Beck, but do not ski down into the very steep-sided valley of this stream.

On the N side of Culter Fell a longer tour starts at Mitchell Hill. An undulating route goes up the N ridge of Cardon Hill, then over King Bank Head, meeting the fence leading to the summit. On the descent from Cardon Hill choose the best route down the northward glens, or down the N ridge, according to the snow conditions.

On the E side of Culter Fell a side road branching off the A701 at Rachan Mill goes up the Holms Water to Glenkirk. A circular tour from there takes in Chapelgill Hill and Leishfoot Hill. This traverse is on short grass and heather, giving good skiing without the need for a deep snow cover. There is a steep corrie on the E side of Culter Fell which should be avoided by skiing S from the summit along a fence towards Moss Law for 1km before dropping E down the shoulder of Leishfoot Hill towards the road end above Glenkirk.

This area of the Border hills is quite different from the Highlands. It may lack the rugged grandeur of the northern mountains, but it has a character of its own, epitomised by the smooth rounded hills which under snow are ideal for ski-touring.

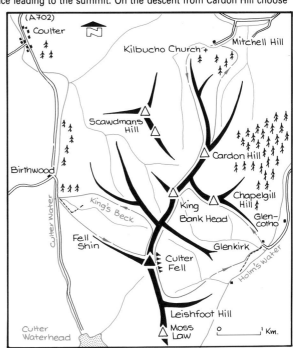

Looking south-east from King's Seat Hill to the Cleish Hills in Fife   *D.J. Bennet*

Several ski tours are possible over the wide flat-topped summits of the Ochil Hills. The longest and most satisfying is the complete traverse from Glen Devon to Sheriff Muir, or vice versa, which is described below. There are also shorter tours, starting for example from Dollar on the south side of the Ochils.

These are hills for the opportunist skier, for when the snow comes it does not usually last for long, and one may have to plan one's tour at short notice. The skiing is mostly easy over gently undulating hills which in summer are entirely grassy, and Nordic skis are suitable. Such is the featureless nature of these hills that a good clear day is desirable, otherwise much time may be spent map reading in bad visibility.

If road conditions permit, leave one car at the Sheriffmuir Inn (827022), or alternatively (if access is blocked by snow) on the A9 road at (843073). Start the traverse from the A823 road in Glen Devon at the Castlehill Reservoir (997033). Follow the farm road to Glenquey, bypassing the farm on the S, and continue along the track on the NW side of the Glenquey Reservoir for ½km, then climb W up to the col S of Bentie Knowe. Continue SW, following the dyke to Whitewisp Hill, then W to Tarmangie Hill. An easy run W leads down to the next col, followed by a level traverse WSW across the flat Skythorn Hill to Andrew Gannel Hill. From there a broad ridge leads W for 1½km to Bencleuch (721m), the highest of the Ochils.

The next section needs accurate navigation, having few identifiable features. Ski WNW from Bencleuch for 4km across a vague col and along the broad ridge to Blairdenon Hill, where three fences meet. Finally, go NW to Mickle Corum, and from there either W over Glentye Hill to Sheriffmuir Inn, or N to the A9 road where one's car has been parked. (23km. 870m. 6-8 hours).

For those wanting a shorter tour, the ascent from Dollar up the edge of the golf course on the W side of the Burn of Sorrow to King's Seat Hill is a short easy climb, which can be extended to Bencleuch over Andrew Gannel Hill. The return is by the same route. (15km. 1000m. 5-6 hours).

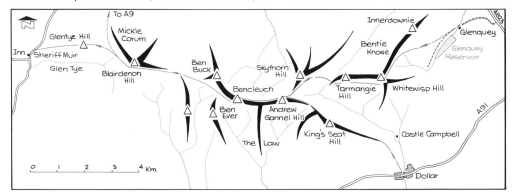

Ben Ledi from Callander   *D.J. Bennet*

Ben Ledi; 879m; (OS Sheet 57; 562098).

Starting points either at Coilantogle Farm (595068) on the A821 road about 4km west of Callander, or at the end of the public road (531076) 1km NNW of Brig o' Turk 10km west of Callander; altitude 110m. Distance 9km. Height climbed 770m. Time 3-4 hours. (Both routes). Rating: ★★/II.

Ben Ledi is a very prominent and accessible hill in a unique position on the southern edge of the Highlands, and it commands extensive views across the Lowlands. It makes a rewarding ski-ascent on a crisp clear day after a heavy snowfall when there is snow cover low down, for the starting points are not much more than 100m above sea level.

One route of ascent starts at Coilantogle Farm and follows the track NW up the hillside towards the SW corner of the forestry plantation. Continue uphill along the W side of the plantation to a short steepening, above which the SE ridge of the hill becomes well defined. Ski easily up the crest of this ridge which has alternate level sections and short steeper rises.

Another route starts 1km NNW of Brig o' Turk at the end of the public road ¼km S of the dam of the Glen Finglas Reservoir. Take the private road which climbs up to the right and follow it high on the E side of the reservoir for 1½km to the farm at the foot of Gleann Casaig. Continue NE up this glen along a hill track high on the SE bank of the stream for a further 1¼km. Then climb due E up the easy-angled hillside which gives a pleasant ascent, steepening at the top where the summit ridge is reached about ¼km NW of the trig point on Ben Ledi.

If the party has two cars, a good traverse can be made by combining the two routes described above.

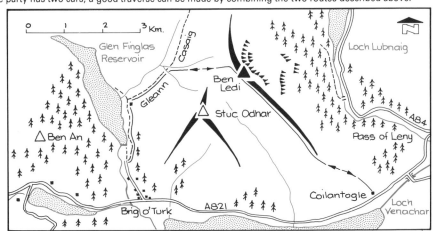

The Luss Hills from The Cobbler   *D.J. Bennet*

Doune Hill; 734m; (OS Sheet 56; 290972).
Beinn Eich; 702m; (OS Sheet 56; 302947).
Beinn Chaorach; 713m; (OS Sheet 56; 287924).
Beinn Tharsuinn; 655m; (OS Sheet 56; (291916).
Beinn a' Mhanaich; 710m; (OS Sheet 56; 269946).
Beinn Bhreac; 681m; (OS Sheet 56; 322000).

The Luss Hills offer a remarkably large area of potentially good ski touring within easy reach of Glasgow. The group is bounded on the east by Loch Lomond, on the south by the minor road through Glen Fruin, and on the west by Loch Long. Access to the hills is possible from points on the Glen Fruin road and the A82 road up Loch Lomond, and also from the roads up Glen Luss and through Glen Douglas from Loch Lomond to Loch Long. Much of the area to the west of The Strone and Beinn a'Mhanaich, and north-west of Doune Hill is used for military purposes and is not accessible.

These hills are remarkably smooth and grassy, with broad ridges and a general absence of crags, screes and boulders, and there are many possible ski tours as the map opposite shows. Since the hills only reach a height of 600-730m, and the starting points are mostly less than 100m above sea-level, good snow cover for skiing is usually obtained only in early winter and is inevitably rather unpredictable. For this reason the descriptions below are confined to suggested ascent routes which give easy access to high ground, some interesting traverses are described, and one or two areas to avoid are mentioned. On good days the views over Loch Lomond, the Firth of Clyde and the Southern Highlands are very fine.

The southern group of hills is usually approached from the Glen Fruin road. There is a good ascent from Ballevoulin farm N up the glen to Beinn Tharsuinn, either on the W side of the burn along the lower slopes of Auchengaich Hill, or up the E side of the burn. A short round tour back to Ballevoulin from Beinn Tharsuinn can be made by traversing E to Pt.693m, then S to Balcnock before skiing down the hillside above Glen Fruin.

Further up Glen Fruin one can start near the bridge over the Auchengaich Burn (273901) and climb the long easy-angled ridge over The Strone to Beinn a' Mhanaich. A descent SE followed by a steep climb in the same direction leads to Beinn Chaorach. Continue SSE, skiing easily along a smooth ridge to Beinn Tharsuinn, descend SSW for 1km along the ridge towards Auchengaich Hill and then ski steeply W down the flank of this hill back to the road at the Auchengaich Burn. (Note that Auchengaich Hill was named Auchenvennel Hill on pre-1986 editions of the OS map).

A longer approach to the southern hills can be made by leaving the main A82 road up Loch Lomond at (353883), 1km N of the B832 road junction, and walking up the private road past Shemore into Glen Finlas. From the head of the reservoir climb NW to Creag an Leinibh, and possibly continue over Pt.693m to Beinn Tharsuinn, returning by Balcnock.

The slopes of the southern hills overlooking Glen Luss are less attractive for skiing as there are areas of very steep ground high up with some crags and deep gullies. However, Creag an Leinibh is accessible from Auchengavin near Luss along the ridge of Coille-eughain Hill. Much further up Glen Luss, 2km beyond Edentaggart farm, there is a good ridge on the N side of the Shieling Burn which leads to Beinn Chaorach.

The hills of the central group are at the head of Glen Luss, and on its N side. Looking up the glen from Luss village, the conical shape of Beinn Eich is very distinctive, with the higher level ridge of Doune Hill behind it. On the N side of the glen the ridge to Beinn Dubh rises directly above Luss, and continues to Mid Hill. It is possible to drive up Glen Luss to the end of the public road near Glenmollochan farm, and there are two or three places where cars can be parked at the roadside nearby.

In good snow conditions the ESE ridge of Beinn Eich gives a very fine ascent, starting up the hillside behind Edentaggart farm. The ridge continues NE and gives easy skiing across a wide col and gradually up to Beinn Lochain and N across a slight dip to Doune Hill. The return by this route enables the skier to stay high for as long as possible before the run down to Glen Luss.

An alternative route to Doune Hill goes along the track on the NE side of the burn in Glen Mollochan, followed by the ascent of the E ridge over the 700m NE top. A descending traverse SSE from the summit leads down to the mid-point of this ascent route. A short tour can be made from Glenmollochan farm up the E side of Glen Striddle to Mid Hill.

On the hills to the N of Glen Douglas there is a good short tour starting at Invergroin farm and going N up Ant-Sreang to the col between Beinn Bhreac and Ben Reoch, from where both hills can be climbed.

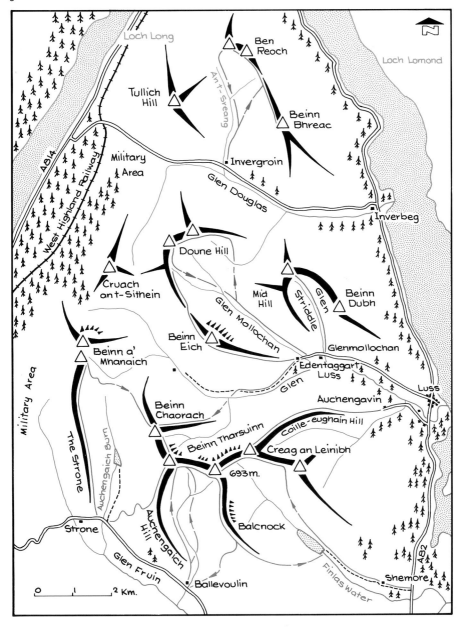

Looking south from Ben Lomond to the islands at the south end of Loch Lomond   *D.J. Bennet*

Ben Lomond; 974m; (OS Sheet 56; 367029).
Starting point at Rowardennan on the east side of Loch Lomond about 10km NNW of Balmaha at (360986); altitude 10m. (Alternative start at Blairvockie farm (377968) 2½km SE of Rowardennan). Distance 13km. Height climbed 970m. Time 4-5 hours. Rating: ★★★/III.

Ben Lomond, well known as one of Scotland's most popular hill-walkers' mountains, is also a surprisingly good skiers' peak. However, as the ascent starts barely 10m above sea-level, it is a ski tour which should be reserved for a day when the snow line is very low. On the whole the skiing on the long middle ridge is easy, but high up the last few hundred metres to the summit are steep and can give good but not unduly difficult skiing. These upper slopes face SW and may therefore show very variable conditions.

The choice of the best starting point will depend on the level of the snow line. If it is above 200m, the simplest start is to carry skis up the well worn path from Rowardennan which leads ENE through the forest onto the open hillside at the foot of the S ridge of Ben Lomond below Sron Aonaich.

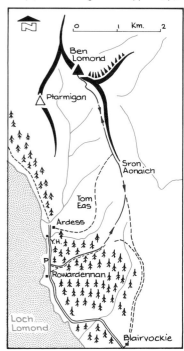

If there is snow down to loch level, then two better approaches are possible which, unlike the path mentioned above, give good skiing at low level. One route starts ¾km N of Rowardennan car park at Ardess cottages, and goes E up the wooded hillside onto the higher open slopes. Above 200m bear N past Tom Eas, then NE to Sron Aonaich. The other starting point is at Blairvockie farm, 2½km SE of Rowardennan. Follow an upland track N to the E of Coille Mhor Hill, and after 2km leave this track and continue N up Sron Aonaich.

Once on the long S ridge of Ben Lomond, where the three routes described converge, there is an easy and in places almost level approach to the upper cone of the mountain. As the ridge begins to steepen, bear NNW (not following the line of the path) and gain height by a rising traverse and a few zig-zags up the SW face. This climb ends on the summit ridge not far from the top, and the last two or three hundred metres go along this narrow ridge and up the short summit dome.

The return is likely to follow more or less the line of ascent, during which you will no doubt have studied the best route for the downhill run. Only the top 200m are steep, and below this there is a long easy schuss along the broad crest of the S ridge.

Skiing along the ridge from Beinn Tulaichean to Cruach Ardrain   D.J. Bennet

Beinn Tulaichean; 946m; (OS Sheet 56; 416196).
Cruach Ardrain; 1046m; (OS Sheets 51 and 56; 409211).
Starting point at the car park at (446184) ¾km east of Inverlochlarig farm, 9km west of Balquhidder; altitude 150m. Distance 12km. Height climbed 1020m. Time 5-6 hours. Rating ★★★/III.

These two mountains to the south-east of Crianlarich are steep, rugged and quite craggy, but despite this they give a very interesting short tour with some good skiing on their upper slopes and along the high ridge connecting them. The approach is from Balquhidder along the narrow road beside Loch Voil, and cars should not be taken beyond the car park ¾km east of Inverlochlarig farm.

Proceed W along the road to the farm where the climb starts directly up the SE slopes of Beinn Tulaichean. The gradient is easy at first, but the hillside steepens and higher up it is necessary to zig-zag to and fro and eventually, as a line of crags high up is approached, make a long rising traverse W to reach the S ridge. Continue up this broad easy-angled ridge, passing a little rocky knoll on the E, and in ¾km reach the summit of Beinn Tulaichean.

Ski NNW down a broad ridge which gives easy running to the col at about 820m, and put on skins for the climb up to Cruach Ardrain. If the snow cover on the ridge leading NNW is poor, it may be better to ski up the shallow gully immediately to its E. At the top of the ridge (or gully) turn right (NE) and climb the last short slope to a little plateau with two cairns. The summit of Cruach Ardrain is 100 metres further NE across a dip.

Return by the ascent route to the 820m col. On the descent the gully will probably give a better run than the ridge, unless the latter is well snow covered. In good conditions, however, the gully gives delightful skiing. From the col it is perfectly feasible to return over Beinn Tulaichean and ski down the ascent route, and this might be the preferred option on a fine afternoon to enjoy the splendid views S and SW to Ben Lomond and the Arrochar Alps.

The alternative, which gives a quicker descent to low ground, is to ski E from the col into the Inverlochlarig Glen. At first the skiing is easy, but lower down the terrain is more broken up by streams, little gullies and crags, and there is no advantage in keeping high on the W side of the glen. If there is snow cover low down, it is best to ski fairly directly down to the track in the glen and enjoy a long easy schuss to Inverlochlarig.

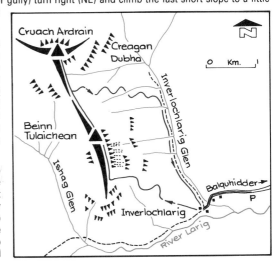

Stob Binnein and Ben More from Stob Coire an Lochain   D.J. Bennet

Stob Binnein; 1165m; (OS Sheet 51; 434226)
Ben More; 1174m; (OS Sheet 51; 432244).
Starting point near the west end of Loch Doine 7½km west of Balquhidder (460192); altitude 150m. Distance 12km. Height climbed 1350m. Time 7-8 hours. Rating: ★★★★/IV.

This is one of the finest ski-traverses in the Scottish mountains, crossing two of the best known and highest peaks of the Southern Highlands. Not only are the scenery and character of the mountains very fine, but the skiing itself is full of interest and in certain conditions may be quite difficult. The traverse follows well-defined ridges which in places are steep-sided and corniced, so this is a route for those who are competent both in skiing and winter mountaineering. In icy conditions or bad weather, and particularly in bad visibility, it is a route which demands great caution. On a fine day, however, it has few equals.

The complete traverse of Stob Binnein and Ben More can be done equally well from S to N, or vice versa. The S to N traverse described here is proably the better choice. It goes up the long S ridge of Stob Binnein over the lower Top of Stob Coire an Lochain, drops 300m to the col, the Bealach-eadar-dha Beinn, between the two peaks, reascends the same height to Ben More and finally descends its NE ridge to Glen Dochart. Variants of this route enable the traverse to be shortened, or a return made to the day's starting point to avoid the need for two cars.

The southern starting point is 7½km W along the road from Balquhidder to Inverlochlarig. Leave the road at the cottage on the W side of the Allt Carnaig and climb NW up Glen Carnaig, crossing two or three small stream-gullies. Pass below the crags on the E side of Stob Invercarnaig and reach the lowest point of the ridge between it and Stob Coire an Lochain by an easy-angled and normally uncorniced slope. Continue NNW up this ridge which becomes steep-sided and corniced on the right, but given adequate snow cover there are no difficulties and it leads directly to Stob Coire an Lochain (1068m).

Beyond this Top the ridge is broad and smooth for a few hundred metres, dropping slightly before rising, increasingly steep and narrow and with a large cornice on the right, towards the summit of Stob Binnein. The last 50m are too steep for skis, and crampons and ice-axe may be needed for the climb to the summit where a small cairn stands at the S edge of the little sloping plateau.

The next section of the traverse may well give the best skiing of the day; equally it may give the most testing. All depends on the state of the snow (or ice) on the NNW face of Stob Binnein. Ski down on the W side of the N ridge, possibly close to the ridge or possibly further W on the broad face of the mountain which drops with unrelenting steepness to the head of the Benmore Burn far below. I have known a complete cover of firm neve which gave an exhilarating yet safe run, and on another occasion a surface of icy snow barely thick enough to cover the stony slope, which gave a most unnerving descent that demanded the utmost caution.

The Bealach-eadar-dha Beinn is a wide flat col with an easy drop on its E side to the head of Coire Chaorach. The ascent to Ben More is steep; N at first onto the ridge, then NE up the ridge, gradually curving round N past some little crags which look prominent from below. The summit is a large crag.

Skiing south from Ben More towards Stob Binnein   D.J. Bennet

The descent of the NE ridge starts easily, skiing along the broad, easy-angled crest, but soon a short rocky step has to be negotiated. Then the skiing is easy again until the ridge narrows at Sron nam Forsairean, where one can either descend SE into Coire Chaorach or continue a descending traverse on the steep NW flank below the rocky crest to regain the ridge in a few hundred metres. Both routes call for care.

The densely planted trees of the Ben More Forest are not far below, and one should aim for a gate in the forest fence about ½km W of the Allt Coire Chaorach. Just below this gate, at (458254), a track goes down through the forest, with a few zig-zags and a crossing of the Allt Coire Chaorach low down before reaching the A85 road in Glen Dochart. With a good snow cover one can ski right down this track, a fitting end to a great day.

It is possible to go direct from the Bealach-eadardha Beinn to Glen Dochart down Coire Chaorach, skiing easily along the NW side of the burn to the tree-line where the traverse route is joined. This is much shorter and easier than the traverse of Ben More. (12km. 1020m. 6 hours).

To return from Ben More to the southern starting point, ski back down the S ridge to the Bealach and then E to the head of Coire Chaorach. If snow conditions are good on the S side of Ben More one can leave the ridge two-thirds of the way down to the Bealach and ski steeply SE between small crags to the head of the corrie, a short and exhilarating run. Once in Coire Chaorach, which forms a level bowl below the E face of Stob Binnein, traverse SE then S with a slight climb to reach the col between Meall na Dige and Stob Coire an Lochain. On the S side of this col a long easy run down the wide open spaces of Glen Carnaig leads back to the starting point. (13½km. 1380m. 7-8 hours).

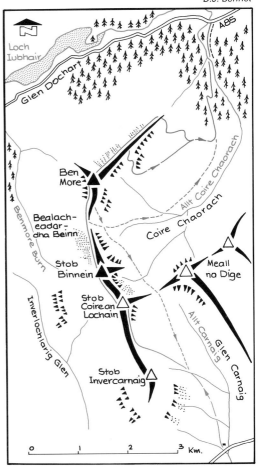

The east face of Stuc a' Chroin

D.J. Bennet

Ben Vorlich; 985m; (OS Sheets 51 and 57; 629189).
Stuc a'Chroin; 975m; (OS Sheets 51 and 57; 617175).
Starting point ⅓km S of Braeleny Farm
(637108) at the end of the public road from
Callander up the glen of the Keltie Water;
altitude 210m.
Distance 19km. Height climbed 1150m. Time 7-
8 hours. Rating: ★★★/IV.

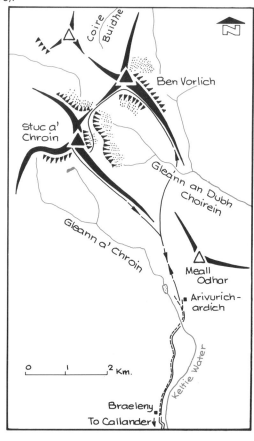

The circuit of these two mountains from the south
is a fine and quite long expedition, the highlight of
which is the traverse from Ben Vorlich to Stuc
a'Chroin. The traverse across the E face of the latter
below a series of steep buttresses and gullies is the
crux and should only be attempted by experienced
mountaineers equipped with ice axes and crampons.
It is, however, an excellent ski-mountaineering
passage in an impressive setting.

From the carpark ⅓km S of Braeleny farm follow
the private road N to the steading at Arivurichardich
where the road ends. The route then continues N
climbing diagonally up the W slopes of Meall Odhar
to the NW end of a broad bealach at the foot of the SE
ridge of Stuc a'Chroin. Easy open slopes then lead
down NE into the Gleann an Dubh Choirein where the
stream is crossed to reach the foot of the S ridge of
Ben Vorlich. For 1km the ridge is broad and easy but
thereafter becomes more steep with several rocky
steps which may be passed on the W. The remains of
old fence posts first appear at a little col on the ridge
and are followed to the summit which has a large
cairn, and 100m to the NW along a level crest there is
also an OS cairn.

From this latter cairn the line of the route follows
the fence posts, descending SW to the Bealach an
Dubh Choirein. From the bealach climb SW, still
following the line of the fence posts towards the foot
of the NE buttress of Stuc a'Chroin. Approaching the

foot of the buttress the terrain becomes rocky and boulder-strewn. At this point bear left and make a rising traverse S for 100 metres to the toe of the buttress where there are many fallen boulders. Continue S below the steep upper rocks of the Stuc making a descending traverse for about 250 metres across a very steep and exposed slope. Great caution is needed and in conditions of hard snow or avalanche risk it would be advisable to take off skis and traverse with ice-axe and crampons. Halfway across the traverse, where the angle eases, ski down more easily to a flat area of huge fallen boulders below the crags.

At that point the difficulties are over. Continue skiing S on a rising traverse along a broad shelf which leads to the SE ridge of Stuc a'Chroin and then turn NW to climb to the summit, turning the steep section of the ridge on the W if the rocks on the crest are not well snow covered.

In good snow conditions the descent down the SE ridge is an excellent run. The route initially follows the uphill tracks but continues on down the ridge which is almost level at two points, to reach the broad bealach of the uphill route. It then follows the outward route down across the W slopes of Meall Odhar to Arivurichardich and finally to Braeleny farm.

There are other shorter and easier ski tours on these two mountains for those who prefer to avoid the difficulties on the E face of Stuc a' Chroin. The ascent of the Stuc itself is most easily done from Braeleny farm by following the route described above to the bealach at the foot of its SE ridge, and climbing along this ridge to the summit. The return by the same way completes an easy tour. (Grade II/III).

The shortest ascent of Ben Vorlich by itself is from Ardvorlich on the south side of Loch Earn. Follow the track S up the W side of Glen Vorlich to the foot of Coire Buidhe and continue in the same direction up the N ridge of Ben Vorlich. The ridge steepens at its top where the W ridge is joined just before the summit. The descent can be varied by skiing W then NW from the summit to the bealach at the head of Coire Buidhe, and then down this corrie to rejoin the uphill route. (Grade III).

The ascent of Stuc a' Chroin from Loch Earn by Glen Ample cannot be recommended as there are extensive recent forestry plantations in this glen, and the NW ridge of the Stuc (by which the ascent might be made) is quite steep and craggy around its flanks.

Stuc a'Chroin from Gleann an Dubh Choirein   G. Mackenzie

Ben Chonzie; 931m; (OS Sheets 51 and 52; 774309). Starting points: (1) In Glen Lednock near Invergeldie farm (740274); altitude 220m. Distance 13km. Height climbed 710m. Time 4-5 hours. (2) In Glen Turret at the Loch Turret dam (821265); altitude 350m. Distance 12km. Height climbed 580m. Time 4 hours. Rating: ★★/II.

One of the nearest Munros to the towns of Central Scotland, Ben Chonzie is deservedly popular. It is very accessible and, whilst not having any notable features, it provides splendid views of the Lawers range, Schiehallion and all the major summits of the Southern Highlands. It is not a good snow-holding mountain late in the season, and because of its abundant heather it requires a firm snow base if good running is to be enjoyed.

If the approach from Comrie by Glen Lednock is chosen, Invergeldie farm is the best starting place and the track going N from there is followed for 1½km on the W side of the Invergeldie Burn to an obvious crossing of the burn below a concrete dam. Follow the shooting track which goes ENE until with ample snow cover it is possible to head NE by steeper slopes to reach the broad ridge of the mountain. Follow the fence NW and then NE to gain the summit cairn.

Ben Chonzie from Invergeldie in Glen Lednock   J.N. Mather

There are two possibilities for the downhill run: either by the ascent route, or by a descent W from the summit to the head of the Invergeldie Burn which is followed downstream until one's uphill tracks are regained.

The alternative route to Ben Chonzie, which gives a more interesting ascent and takes one into the crag-girt E corrie above Lochan Uaine, is from Glen Turret. Taking the private road from Crieff up to the Loch Turret dam, continue along the track on the NE side of the loch until, near its head, the track begins to climb uphill. Continue near the loch-side past the rhododendrons of the old lodge to the head of the loch. From there start an easy climb WNW diagonally across the hillside below small crags, and continue in the same direction up the big east-facing corrie until the summit ridge is reached not far SW of the summit.

The traverse of Ben Chonzie by the two routes described is the best expedition, but it requires two cars or a helpful non-skiing driver. The featureless character of the mountain makes accurate navigation essential in bad weather, particularly if the snow is deep enough to bury the fence posts along the summit ridge.

A word of warning may be given about skiing across frozen lochs and reservoirs in conditions of hard frost when they may be expected to be safe. If, as may well be the case with reservoirs, water has been drawn down and not replaced naturally by streams, the surface ice may be unsupported and much thinner than one might expect, and consequently dangerous to ski across.

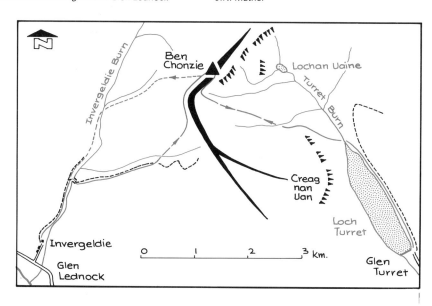

Schiehallion from the north-west   *D.J. Bennet*

Schiehallion; 1083m; (OS Sheet 51; 714548).
Starting point near Braes of Foss farm on the Coshieville to Kinloch Rannoch road at a Forestry Commission car park at (753557); altitude 330m. Distance 9km. Height climbed 760m. Time 4 hours. Rating: ★★/III.

An isolated and fine looking peak from any angle, Schiehallion is both bouldery and heathery, and is only worth attempting on skis when there is ample snow cover. Given such conditions, it provides a good though short expedition in impressive surroundings.

The starting point beside the road on the north-side of the mountain near Braes of Foss is marked by a cairn and plaque to commemorate the work of the one-time Astronomer Royal. Take the path which leads through the forest and along the edge of the trees onto the open hillside, and continue WSW over slopes which become steeper as you approach the E ridge of the mountain. The ridge is reached at about 800m, and it is then simply a case of following it to the summit. Without a good covering of snow the boulder strewn crest may be difficult to ski, and recourse to better snow on its N side may be necessary.

The downhill run may well be dictated by the need to return to one's starting point, so the E ridge again provides the route and while the spine of the ridge may prove difficult to ski if the boulders are not well snow covered, good easy skiing can be enjoyed on either side just below the crest.

Lower down it is probably best to leave the ridge at a fairly level place about 300 metres W of the point where it was gained on the uphill route, and descend ENE by a wide steep slope directly above the headwaters of the burn which flows down to Braes of Foss. By trending right and keeping to the true right bank of the burn you can use the north-facing slopes which may well have the best snow cover and enable you to ski right back to the starting point. Alternatively, you can descend the ridge for a further 300 or 400 metres to find easier skiing close to the line of ascent.

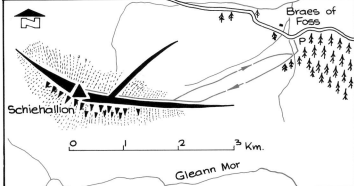

The Carn Mairg group from the south   *C.R. Ford*

Carn Gorm; 1028m; (OS Sheet 51; 635501).
Meall Garbh; 968m; (OS Sheet 51; 646517).
Carn Mairg; 1041m; (OS Sheet 51; 684513).
Creag Mhor; 981m; (OS Sheet 51; 695496).
Starting point at Invervar, Glen Lyon (665483); altitude 190m. Distance 17km. Height climbed 1300m. Time 7 hours. Rating: ★★★/III.

This tour provides an interesting high level traverse around the horseshoe of hills situated on the north side of Glen Lyon. It has the added incentive of taking in four "ski-Munros" without too much effort as there is little height loss between summits. A generous snow cover, although not essential, will limit the amount of ski-sole to be left behind on the boulders which abound along sections of the traverse.

Park the car a few metres down the side road to Dericambus opposite Invervar approximately 8km W of Fortingall. The traverse can be done either clockwise or anti-clockwise and the wind direction may dictate which option is chosen (this particular group of hills seems to attract strong winds). If required the tour can be cut short from almost any point along its length by descending to Invervar. The following describes the traverse in the clockwise direction, i.e. ascending Carn Gorm initially.

Follow the track which starts on the E side of the road bridge over the Invervar Burn, N through the forest to emerge after 400 metres. Continue up the track following the E bank of the burn for 1km before crossing a footbridge to reach the nothernmost point of the forestry plantation on the W side of the burn where the fence takes an acute bend. Ascend open slopes to gain the SE ridge of Carn Gorm and then follow the ridge more steeply to the summit cairn.

The descent off Carn Gorm provides a good run with just under 200m height drop to the col W of An Sgorr. Ski down the NNE ridge initially, then move E below its crest for the, generally, better snow. The minor top of An Sgorr can be avoided by skirting its NW side.

Put skins back on and ascend NE to reach the line of old fenceposts which should then be followed E to the more northerly of Meall Garbh's two summit cairns – the conscientious may wish to visit both. Continue E along the line of rusting fenceposts (which are at their best when masked by fog-crystals) over Meall a'Bharr before turning SE and ascending the narrower, and bouldery, ridge leading to the main summit of the traverse – Carn Mairg. Although the skiing over this section is not too spectacular, it is compensated for by the superb views of Schiehallion to the N and the Lawers group to the S.

From Carn Mairg descend E, avoiding boulders and small rocky outcrops, for about ⅓km and then turn SSE to reach the col at about 840m. The final ascent of the traverse is then SSE up the broad slope which leads to the rocky tor forming the main top of Creag Mhor.

The wide snowfields of the Carn Mairg range   *D.J. Bennet*

The slopes to the N of Creag Mhor's W ridge tend to hold snow well and should be descended to reach the Allt Coir'Chearcail close to the small bothy at (673498). Even when the slopes adjacent to the stream are bare, a ribbon of snow often clings to its banks giving a convenient descent route to the confluence with the Invervar Burn where the outward route is rejoined for the short descent through the forest to Invervar.

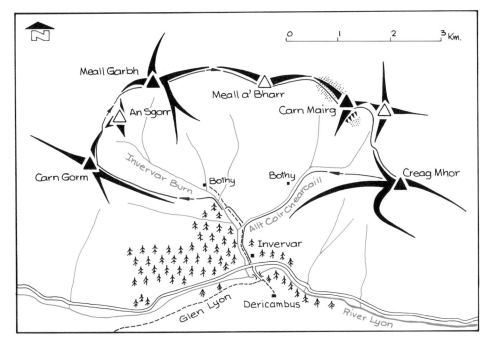

Ben Lawers and Beinn Ghlas from the south ridge of Meall Corranaich   D.J. Bennet

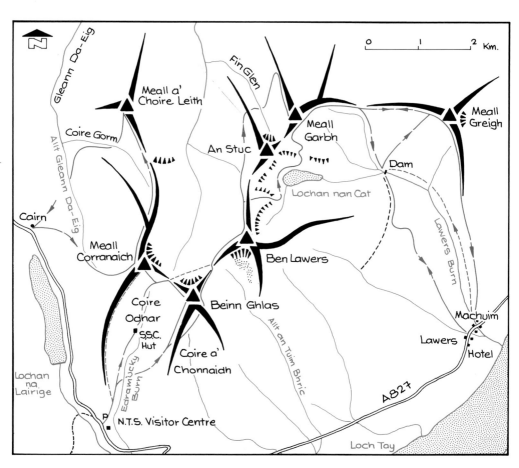

Skiing off Meall Corranaich towards Coire Odhar   *D.J. Bennet*

Among the Scottish mountains, Ben Lawers is rightly regarded by ski-mountaineers as being one of the very best. It is not a single peak, but a great range of six distinct mountains, linked by high ridges and surrounded by many corries. The relative absence of crags and boulder fields, and the predominance of smooth grassy slopes make Ben Lawers an ideal skiers' mountain, for with only a modest cover of snow skiing is possible, and with a complete cover it is superb. This, combined with the varied and interesting topography of the range, makes possible a great variety of ski tours from the simple ascent of a single peak to the traverse of the whole massif. Here it is only possible to describe a few of the many possibilities.

The most popular starting point for skiing on Ben Lawers is the car park at the National Trust for Scotland Visitor Centre 2½km along the narrow road from Loch Tay to Glen Lyon. This point is at the foot of Coire Odhar, and 2km up the corrie the long-established hut of the Scottish Ski Club is a reminder that Ben Lawers was once the focus of Scottish skiing. Another slightly higher starting point for tours to the west end of the range is at the prominent cairn on the same road, ½km N of the N end of Lochan na Lairige. This road is not kept open in winter, and in conditions of deep snow it would be impossible to drive up to the points just mentioned. A third point of access to Ben Lawers is the little village of Lawers, climbing up by the Lawers Burn towards Lochan nan Cat.

In the following descriptions three relatively short tours and the traverse of the whole range are described as being typical of the variety of skiing on this grand mountain.

Meall Corranaich; 1069m; (OS Sheet 51; 616410).
Meall a'Choire Leith; 926m; (OS Sheet 51; 612439).
Starting point at the cairn on the road from Loch Tay to Glen Lyon at (593417) ½km N of Lochan na Lairige; altitude 550m. Distance 9km. Height climbed 700m. Time 4-5 hours. Rating: ★★★/II.

The traverse of these two hills at the W end of the Ben Lawers range is a fairly short day, particularly if the start is made at the cairn on the road N of Lochan na Lairige. From that point one should head SE, skiing up the shallow corrie at the head of the Allt Gleann Da-Eig rather than up the steep W slopes of Meall Corranaich itself. Near the head of the corrie bear round NE to reach the flat top of Meall Corranaich where the small cairn is near the NE edge of the little summit plateau.

Ski down the broad, easy-angled N ridge, being careful in bad visibility to keep to the E of the upper part of Coire Gorm at the point where the ridge divides after 1km. From the col (c.780m) 1km further on there is a short climb of 150m to the flat summit of Meall a' Choire Leith.

Ski S from the summit into the upper part of Coire Gorm. This corrie, known in the skiing fraternity as Charlie's Gully, often holds snow well and gives a pleasant run for a kilometre or so. Do not go right down to the junction with the Allt Gleann Da-Eig, but make a traverse SW across rough ground, regaining a little height to cross the flat col at (596419) close to the cairn at the starting point.

Skiing off Beinn Ghlas towards Ben Lawers   *D.J. Bennet*

Beinn Ghlas; 1103m; (OS Sheet 51; 626404).
Ben Lawers; 1214m; (OS Sheet 51; 636414).
Starting point at the NTS Visitor Centre car park (609377); altitude 440m. Distance 11km. Height climbed (max) 1070m. Time 5-6 hours. Rating: ★★★★/IV.

This is an excellent and popular tour, showing the best of Ben Lawers without being unduly long. Ski up Coire Odhar, possibly following the track on the W side of the Edramucky Burn if snow cover elsewhere is thin. The choice of the best route up Beinn Ghlas depends on the snow conditions on its SW side. One can either (a) continue up the W side of the burn past the Ski Club hut to the col at the head of the corrie and climb the NW ridge of Beinn Ghlas, or (b) cross to the E side of the burn and ski up onto the SSW ridge and follow it to the summit, or (c) continue across the SSW ridge into the shallow Coire a' Chonnaidh and ski steeply up its head onto the SSE ridge.

From the summit of Beinn Ghlas ski down the broad crest of the NE ridge. In good conditions this is an easy run, but in bad visibility care is needed as the flanks of the ridge are steep. This run ends at the col below Ben Lawers, and the next part of the ridge upwards is steep and rocky; carrying skis may be necessary for a short distance. Higher up the slope becomes smooth, and it is possible to ski right up to the big summit cairn.

Looking round from this lofty point there are many tempting downhill runs, not least the steep and exciting 500m descent NE to Lochan nan Cat, or the equally steep run S to the head of Allt an Tuim Bhric. These are routes for competent skiers in good conditions.

For those returning to Coire Odhar, however, the outward route over Beinn Ghlas is probably the best choice, and there is good skiing, first down the SW ridge of Ben Lawers to the col (keeping to the NW side of the ridge), and finally off Beinn Ghlas into Coire Odhar. It is possible to avoid the reascent of Beinn Ghlas by traversing from the col below its N face on a slightly downhill run across the corrie to the col at the head of Coire Odhar. From there a straight run downhill past the Ski Club hut leads to the car park.

Meall Greigh; 1001m; (OS Sheet 51; 674437).
Meall Garbh; 1118m; (OS Sheet 51; 644437).
Starting point at Lawers village on the A827 road; altitude 190m. Distance 14km. Height climbed 1110m. Time 5-6 hours. Rating: ★★★/II.

The north-east end of the Lawers range opens out between Meall Garbh and Meall Greigh to form a broad ridge on the north side of the Lawers Burn, and the traverse of these two hills is a good and fairly easy ski tour. On a fine day it gives superb views of the great craggy faces of Ben Lawers and An Stuc above Lochan nan Cat, the most impressive part of the range.

One can start either at the Lawers Hotel on the W side of the Lawers Burn, or at the road leading to Machuim farm on the E side. Both ways lead NNW through fields and onto the open hillside, and one comes eventually to a small dam on the Lawers Burn at 600m (663427). Going to Meall Greigh first, ski NE up the open hillside, choosing one of the snow-filled stream beds which lead up to the broad ridge just W of the summit.

The final climb to the summit of Ben Lawers   *D.J. Bennet*

Ski W along the very broad ridge, easy going in good conditions, but calling for accurate navigation in cloud, to reach the 830m col below Meall Garbh. The ascent of this hill goes up an obvious gully, usually well filled with snow, or up the slopes to its left or right, to reach the NW ridge which leads easily to the cairn of Meall Garbh. The continuation of the main ridge SW is narrow, and there is a fine view along it to An Stuc and Ben Lawers. An Stuc is the only peak of the range which cannot be easily traversed on skis.

Return by the ascent route to the 830m col, and from there ski down to the Lawers Burn dam by an easy run. Below the dam there is at least 3km more skiing down wide open slopes, and a thin snow cover on the fields above Lawers Hotel is sufficient for a long schuss down to the road.

The Grand Traverse
Starting point at the cairn on the Loch Tay to Glen Lyon road at (593417) ½km N of Lochan na Lairige; altitude 550m. Distance 20km. Height climbed 1550m. Time 8-10 hours. Rating: ★★★★★/IV.

The traverse of Ben Lawers range is undoubtedly one of the three or four best ski-mountaineering expeditions in Scotland, giving a day of extraordinary variety and interest, both as regards skiing and scenery. It links up parts of the three shorter tours just described and, dependent on the route chosen, it gives some challenging ski-runs. The best direction is from SW to NE, and an essential member of the party is a friendly driver who will take the car from the starting point near Lochan na Lairige to the finishing point at Lawers village. Finally, choose good conditions for the traverse, and you will be sure to have a day that will be the equal of any in your skiing experience.

From the cairn N of Lochan na Lairige take the route described above to Meall Corranaich. Alternatively, one can start at the NTS Visitor Centre and ski up the S ridge of the hill without difficulty, given adequate snow cover. Ski steeply down from Meall Corranaich by the SSE face into the head of Coire Odhar, traverse E to the col at the head of the corrie and climb the NW ridge of Beinn Ghlas. Continue along the ridge to Ben Lawers as described above.

The next section of the main ridge between Ben Lawers and Meall Garbh leads past An Stuc, a steep, rocky peak which skiers must bypass on one side or the other. One way is to ski N from Ben Lawers, slightly on the W side of the ridge past the rocky knoll of Stob an Fhithich, and continue still bearing N on a descending traverse across the W flank of An Stuc. The N ridge of that peak is reached overlooking the head of the Fin Glen and a short but very steep descent has to be made into this corrie. (The ridge may be corniced on its E side, but there is usually at least one place where this cornice is discontinuous). Ski down to a big boulder at about 720m in the Fin Glen and there put on skins for the ascent to Meall Garbh, first by an ascending traverse NE to reach the NW ridge, then up that ridge.

The alternative route from Ben Lawers to Meall Garbh goes down the N ridge for ¾km to the flattening before Stob an Fhithich. There turn right and ski steeply E on a diagonal descent (beware of the precipitous drop on the downhill side) until a clear route appears down to Lochan nan Cat. Contour round the N side of the lochan and climb steeply to Meall Garbh.

The last part of the traverse reverses the route already described for Meall Greigh, but from the top of that hill it is probably best to ski due S, more or less directly to Machuim farm, as this gives a quicker descent than crossing to the W side of the Lawers Burn.

On the ridge from Meall nan Tarmachan towards Meall Garbh   *D.J. Bennet*

Meall nan Tarmachan; 1043m; (OS Sheet 51; 585390).
Starting point on the road from Loch Tay to Glen Lyon at (604383) 1km south of the Lochan na Lairige dam; altitude 460m. Distance 8km. Height climbed 590m. Time 3-4 hours. Rating: ★★★/III.

The craggy outline of the Tarmachan Hills as seen from Killin does not at first suggest that they are good skiers' mountains, but closer acquaintance may well change this impression, for there are some good snow-holding corries to the N and S of the knolly summit ridge. Meall nan Tarmachan, the highest, is the most accessible of the four peaks of this group, and it gives an interesting little ski tour, very suitable for a short winter's day.

The starting point is about ½km NW of the Ben Lawers Visitor Centre on the road from Loch Tay to Glen Lyon, but in deep snow it may not be possible to reach this point by car as the road is not kept open in winter. From this point climb or ski WSW up the flank of Meall nan Tarmachan's S ridge, and cross the broad crest of this ridge to enter the shallow corrie at the head of the Allt Tir Artair. Ski N up the E tributary of this burn, which usually holds snow well, to its head where a few fence posts may be useful landmarks in mist.

Ahead, to the NW, the upper slopes of Meall nan Tarmachan steepen considerably, forming a wide gully which may be corniced at its top. Ski up for about 60m, then (to avoid the very steep upper slope and the cornice at the top) traverse right (NE) along a broad rising terrace under crags. This gives a fine route across the E face just below the summit, debouching a short distance NE of the cairn. The last few metres along the ridge are easy.

It is quite possible to ski down by the ascent route, but a steeper and more sporting run can be had by skiing S from the cairn for about 200 metres to the top of the gully which (lower down) was used on the ascent. The cornice is seldom completely overhanging, and it may be possible to get an exciting descent for 60m to rejoin the uphill route, and follow it down.

For those who want a longer day, two possibilities exist to extend the tour. One can ski easily SW from Meall nan Tarmachan down the broad summit ridge to the tiny lochans below Meall Garbh (1026m) and climb on foot to that sharp pointed summit. Alternatively, one can ski NW into Coire Riadhailt down steep slopes which hold snow well and give a fine descent of 200m, but beware of small crags not easily seen from above. Once easy ground is reached, put on skins and climb E over the NE ridge of Meall nan· Tarmachan and finally make a descending traverse SE across a steep hillside with small crags to return to the day's starting point.

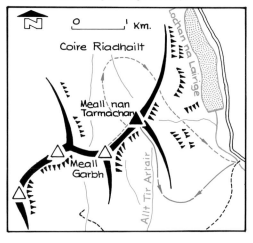

On the descent from Meall Ghaordie, looking east to Ben Lawers   D.J. Bennet

Meall Ghaordie; 1039m; (OS Sheet 51; 514397).
Starting point just west of Duncroisk farm in Glen Lochay (527363); altitude 150m. Distance 8km. Height climbed 890m. Time 3-4 hours. Rating: ★★/II.

   Meall Ghaordie, situated to the north of Glen Lochay about 10 kilometres north-west of Killin, has been described by an elderly Munro-bagger, possibly somewhat optimistically, as being a 'ninety minute Munro'. Although it may not be the most inspiring of summits, and its distance from any neighbouring Munros makes a longer traverse of two or three mountains impracticable, it does make an excellent short outing on skis without being too demanding of time, effort or expertise.

   As with most ski tours, it is always an advantage if there is good snow cover down to the road. On the writer's ascent, however, the snow line was at approximately 500m, but it was still possible to put on skis and skins just above the road and ascend along a strand of snow beside one of the burns to the W of Duncroisk.

   From a point on the road just W of the bridge over the Allt Dhuin Croisg ascend virtually due N to gain the easy slopes of the broad SE shoulder. A direct line can then be taken for the summit which lies just beyond and above some small rock outcrops.

   A recommended variation for the descent is to ski down slightly to the E of the summit before entering the shallow corrie formed by the most westerly tributary of the Allt Dhuin Croisg. This gives a fine run down to the main stream near a sheepfank, from where a track above the W bank of the stream may be followed back to the road. Alternatively, if there is sufficient snow, the line of ascent can be reversed.

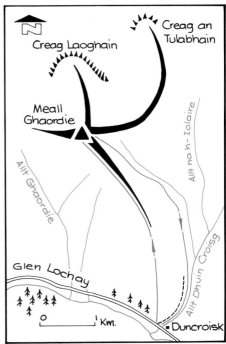

The summit of Stuchd an Lochain from the east   C.R. Ford

Stuchd an Lochain; 960m; (OS Sheet 41; 483448).
Starting point in Glen Lyon at the bridge over the Allt Conait (530446) about 5km west of Bridge of Balgie; altitude 250m. Distance 10km. Height climbed 720m. Time 5-6 hours. Rating: ★★★/III.

Stuchd an Lochain is rather an isolated mountain lying far up Glen Lyon, separated from its neighbours by that glen and the deep trench holding Loch an Daimh to its north. It gives an interesting ski ascent by its east ridge, with magnificent views in clear weather, but a good snow cover is needed to make the rough lower ground skiable.

From the road in Glen Lyon at the Allt Conait ascend W over undulating ground to the Allt Ruighe Ghiubhas, aiming to reach the burn at its confluence with the stream flowing out of Coire an Duich. This corrie is not recommended as a ski route for the headwall is steep and may be corniced. Cross the burn and bear W to the foot of the steepening E ridge of Stuchd an Lochain. Ascend this by a very shallow gully, turning the steeper section by a traverse left, then regain the ridge at the fence along its crest. Follow this to the E top, Sron Chona Choirein.

The summit ridge is broad and undulating, and should hold enough snow to give a pleasant traverse above Lochan nan Cat to the foot of the final peak. Note the cairn on a rise approximately half way along the ridge. The last hundred metres to the summit is steep and may not be skiable.

On the descent return to the cairn half way along the ridge to Sron Chona Choirein, and from there make a descending traverse ESE across a broad smooth snowfield which should provide good skiing down to the foot of the E ridge. From there pick the best route through the drumlins along the Allt Ruighe Ghiubhas back to the starting point.

If the party has two cars, a finer tour can be made by continuing the traverse from the summit SW down the Allt Camaslaidh to Pubil, 8km up the road from the starting point at the Allt Conait. The run down the Allt Camaslaidh is quite easy, particularly in its shallow upper basin.

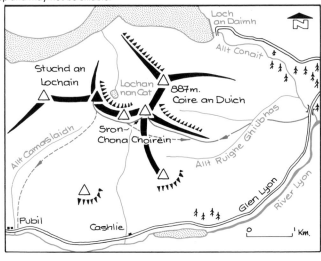

On Beinn Heasgarnich, looking north-east to Stuchd an Lochain   *R. Simpson*

Creag Mhor; 1048m; (OS Sheets 50 and 51; 390361).
Beinn Heasgarnich; 1076m; (OS Sheet 51; 413383).
Starting point at the end of the public road up Glen Lochay at (466364); altitude 220m. Distance 20km. Height climbed 1260m. Time 7-8 hours. Rating: ★★★/III.

These two hills lie several kilometres west of the end of the public road up Glen Lochay. They both usually hold snow well, and Beinn Heasgarnich in particular has an extensive area of high corries and broad ridges. The traverse of these two hills is a fine expedition, but rather long as one has to walk along the private road in Glen Lochay for 5km to reach the foot of Creag Mhor (unless one is lucky enough to have permission to drive along this road to Batavaime). Beinn Heasgarnich by itself is a relatively short tour, particularly if one is able to drive to the summit of the road which leads from Kenknock in Glen Lochay northwards to Glen Lyon. The summit of that road is at 520m, and the ascent from there to Beinn Heasgarnich up the Coire Ban Mor is easy.

For the traverse of the two hills, however, walk or (if the snow cover is low enough) ski along the rough private road to Batavaime cottage. From there start a gentle ascending traverse W round the foot of Sron nan Eun into Coire-cheathaich at about 550m where two possible routes diverge. The simplest is to continue the curving ascent NW onto the ridge between Sron nan Eun and Creag Mhor, and then go along this easy ridge to the promiment cairn on Creag Mhor. The second choice is to continue up Coire-cheathaich, passing below the impressive craggy slopes on the NE face of Stob nan Clach (958m), to the bealach ½km SW of Creag Mhor which is easily reached up a broad ridge.

The NE face of Creag Mhor is too steep and rocky for skiing, so it is essential to ski NW from the summit for ½km, then turn N down the Meall Tionail ridge for ¾km until it becomes fairly level at about 820m. At that point ski off the ridge SSE down an easy-angled corrie to the bealach at Lochan na Baintighearna (which will probably be hidden under snow). The SW ridge of Beinn Heasgarnich rises steeply above this wide flat col.

The most direct route of ascent starts as a rising traverse up the N flank of the ridge, and higher up one can either aim to reach the ridge 1km S of Beinn Heasgarnich, or continue the rising traverse direct to the summit. This north-facing slope is steep enough to be potentially dangerous in unstable snow conditions, but otherwise it should pose no problems. If it is considered to be too steep or unsafe, a traverse from Lochan na Baintighearna bearing ESE for just over 1km below rough ground gives access to easy slopes which can be climbed N to reach the broad S ridge of Beinn Heasgarnich 1km S of the summit.

The return to the public road-end in Glen Lochay involves at least 5km of skiing, much of it easy-angled, and good route selection is necessary to maintain the downhill momentum. The most direct route is a long descending traverse, SE at first, then E across the vast southern flank of Beinn Heasgarnich. Alternatively, one can ski E down Coire Ban Mor and along the Allt Tarsuinn to reach the road between Glen Lochay and Glen Lyon, and end the day by skiing or walking down this road to Glen Lochay.

If returning to Batavaime, there is an excellent run SW from the south top to the junction of streams at 600m, then SE down the right bank of the Allt Batavaim.
Map on page 33.

The ascent to Sgiath Chuil above the Allt Riobain   C.R. Ford

Sgiath Chuil; 935m; (OS Sheet 51; 463318).
Meall Glas; 960m; (OS Sheet 51; 431322).
Starting point in Glen Dochart on the A85 road at (448276) ½km south of Auchessan farm; altitude 160m. Distance 16km. Height climbed 1220m. Time 6-7 hours.
Alternative starting point in Glen Lochay at the end of the public road at (466364); altitude 220m. Distance 16km. Height climbed 1200m. Time 6-7 hours. Rating: ★★/IV (III by easier route).

These two hills lie between Glen Dochart and Glen Lochay, and can be climbed from either glen. The southern approach from Glen Dochart is probably the more popular route because of its easy accessibility from the A85 road, and if there is a good snow cover down to the glen it is a perfectly good route. If the snow cover on the southern slopes is thin, or the snow line a long way above the glen, then the Glen Lochay approach may have the advantage of better snow cover on the north facing slopes.

The circular traverse of these hills may be done in either direction, but it is probably better to ski down the west slopes of Meall a' Churain which give a fine steep run, and then climb up the east side of Beinn Cheathaich which, being rather rough and studded with boulders gives less satisfactory skiing. In hard icy conditions the steep sections of these slopes, if taken direct, may require ice-axe and crampons, but they can be avoided by detours to the north.

From the A85 in Glen Dochart at (448276) take the private road across the river to Auchessan farm, behind which the open hillside is reached. Climb the slopes between the rock outcrops of Creag nan Uan and the Allt Riobain for about 2km, then bear NE towards Sgiath Chrom, heading for the little shallow corrie between that knoll and the rocky prow of Sgiath Chuil. Finally avoid the steep S face of Sgiath Chuil by a rising traverse across the W side of the peak and reach the summit from that side.

Traverse N along the fairly level ridge to Meall a' Churain (918m). The direct descent W from that Top gives a very steep and exciting run with a drop of 300m ending at the broad bealach at the head of the Allt Riobain. Alternatively, if this descent threatens to be too exciting, ski N along the ridge for about ½km to about 700m and then make a descending traverse SW to the bealach. This is an easier and safer descent, particularly in icy or avalanche-prone conditions. (grade III).

Climb Beinn Cheathaich (937m), keeping to the N of the steep rocky slopes immediately below the summit, which is approached up the last hundred metres of the N ridge. Ski easily SW then W along the broad ridge to Meall Glas. From that summit, if you are returning to Glen Dochart, return ESE, more or less along the uphill track, for about 300 metres, then bear SE and ski down a steep slope which provides the only feasible ski run through the rocky escarpment on the S side of the hill. It is important, and possibly rather difficult in bad visibility, to find the correct descent route, as any error to the E or W may lead one onto steep ground that will force you to take off skis and climb down. However, on the correct route the angle soon eases and the run continues without difficulty, following the general line of the streams which flow SE towards the Allt Riobain where the uphill tracks are rejoined.

The starting point on the Glen Lochay side of the hills is at the end of the public road in the glen just W of Kenknock farm. Walk or ski W along the private road for 1½km and cross the river to Lubchurran. Climb the broad ridge on the E side of the Lubchurran Burn to Meall a' Churain where the above route is joined. Continue by this route to Meall Glas. The descent from there to Glen Lochay goes down the wide concave bowl of Coire Cheathaich, which usually holds snow well in its upper part. If the snow cover is good, you will enjoy a steep run N from the summit followed by a long diagonal schuss NE across the corrie for 3km, with a descent of 600m or more, towards Lubchurran.

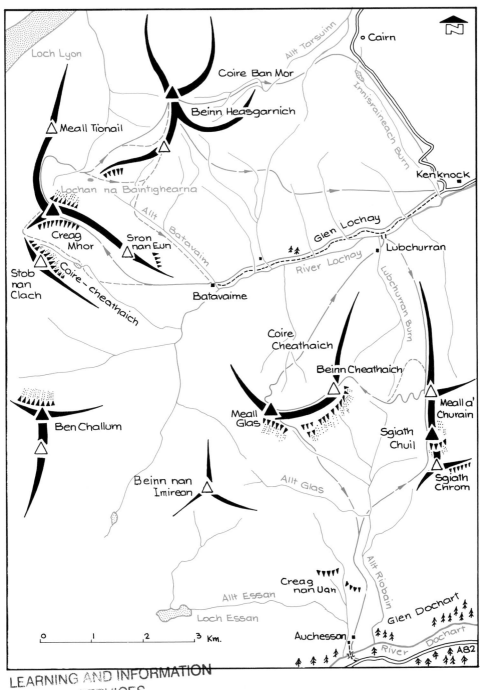

The ascent to Beinn Dubhchraig at the foot of Coire Dubhchraig   *G. Mackenzie*

Beinn a' Chleibh; 916m; (OS Sheet 50; 251256).
Ben Lui; 1130m; (OS Sheet 50; 266263).
Ben Oss; 1029m; (OS Sheet 50; 287253).
Beinn Dubhchraig; 978m; (OS Sheet 50; 308255).
Starting point at a parking place in Glen Lochy beside the A85 road at (239278); altitude 190m.
Distance 19km. Height climbed 1650m. Time 7-8 hours. Rating: ★★★★/III.

This splendid group of mountains provides one of the best ski tours in Scotland. Individually Ben Lui and Beinn Dubhchraig provide very good tours, but ski tourers with sufficient stamina to cope with 1650m of climbing on skins will wish to complete the traverse of all four mountains. This may be undertaken in either direction but as the finest downhill runs are on the W to E traverse, this is the direction described.

From the car park ford the River Lochy just upstream from the point where the Eas Daimh flows into it. As there are no stepping stones, some parties may prefer to walk 1km downriver to a footbridge (not shown on the OS map). On the S side of the river follow a good path on the N side of the Eas Daimh through the forest. In 0.6km cross the Eas Daimh and climb close to the stream which drains the Fionn Choirein. Due to the steep hillside and the proximity of the forest to the stream, in places it may be necessary to carry skis for a short distance. At the top of the forest the angle eases and the deer fence is crossed at a stile close to the stream.

Continue straight up the corrie to reach the headwall, which, although not excessively steep, does have several small rocky outcrops which may be avoided by a left to right traverse finishing exactly on the col. Although it need not form part of the traverse, it is satisfying to climb 140m WSW to the summit of Beinn a'Chleibh and then return to the col.

From the col the climb up the SW ridge of Ben Lui is straightforward for 240m above which the ridge is both steeper and rocky. To avoid the rocks traverse to the right for 100 metres then ascend in the same direction to join the SE ridge not far from the summit. The summit is an excellent viewpoint, particularly if there are parties in the Central Gully.

From the summit there is an exhilarating run of 420m down the SE ridge. Some care is required, however, particularly when the snow on the crest of the ridge is confined to the E edge which is precipitous. The col at the foot of the ridge is wide with several hillocks which could be confusing in bad visibility.

From the col ascend E then NE, gaining 200m up an undulating ridge to reach the steeper summit cone of Ben Oss. Turn N and climb 100m to reach the summit. From there ski down a gently inclined ridge NNE to a small col followed by a short climb to the E (avoid putting on skins). The final slope down to the next col follows a long scoop which holds snow well.

The W shoulder of Beinn Dubhchraig which rises to the E of the col is rocky and requires a good covering snow for an easy ascent. Once on top of this shoulder turn SE to climb the final ridge to the summit.

Ben Lui from Ben Oss   *D.J. Bennet*

In good snow conditions the descent from the summit of Beinn Dubhchraig down Coire Dubhchraig to the Old Caledonian pinewood at its foot is a very fine long run, although recent forestry plantings in the lower half of the corrie will inevitably spoil it in due course.

Ski steeply N from the summit and soon reach easier slopes at the head of the Allt Coire Dubhchraig. Continue easily in long schusses down the NW side of this stream, crossing three fences, and ski through the pinewood to a footbridge at its NE corner. Two hundred metres E of this bridge a track leads over the railway and down to the A82 road in Strathfillan.

Finally, one has to retrieve the car left in Glen Lochy. A second car, a friendly driver to give a lift or the Glasgow to Oban bus are three possible solutions to this problem.

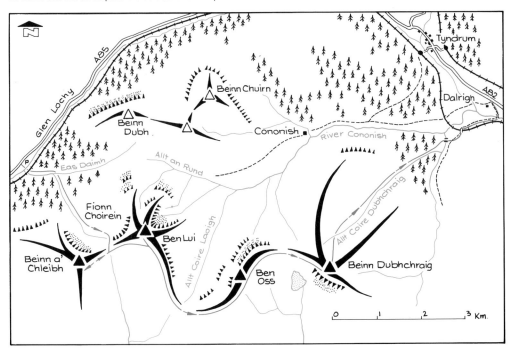

Descent from Ben Challum towards Strath Fillan   *C.R. Ford*

Ben Challum; 1025m; (OS Sheet 50; 387323).
Starting point at Kirkton farm in Strath Fillan (359284); altitude 170m. Distance 11km. Height climbed 960m. Time 4 hours. Rating: ★★/II.

Ben Challum rises on the north-east side of Strath Fillan between Crianlarich and Tyndrum. Its appearance from the strath is rather uninspiring, characterised by the wide lower slopes rising at an easy angle. Above them is the rounded dome of the South Top, beyond which the summit is hidden.

Despite its rather uninteresting appearance, Ben Challum gives a pleasant ascent on skis with good slopes for the downhill run. It is one of the easiest of the Crianlarich hills for the skier, and in good conditions poses no problems. Only the last part of the ridge between the South Top and the summit is at all narrow and exposed. The only other problem might be route-finding in bad visibility, for the south-west side of the mountain is remarkably featureless. On a fine day, however, this is a short and easy tour with grand views of the surrounding mountains.

Kirkton farm is probably the best starting point, and with permission one can park a car at the farm. Follow the track past the old St. Fillan's graveyard and cross the railway at a gate just beyond it. Once on the hill there is no clearly defined route, and one's choice is dictated by the best snow cover. Possibly it is best to keep slightly NW of the steepest rise, looking for gates through the fences which cross the hillside. After an easy climb to about 650m one passes W of a knoll on the ridge and crosses another fence to reach a broad flat col below the upper slopes of Ben Challum.

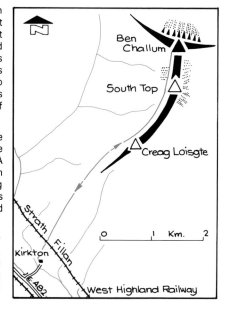

In bad visibility a line of fence posts rising above the NE side of this col may be a useful guide. In clear weather, however, one can ski anywhere up the very broad ridge to the South Top. A few metres W of this top there is a narrow level hollow, and on its W side the ridge continues, dropping slightly and then rising more steeply to the large summit cairn. In good conditions it is quite possible to ski along this ridge, but if there is a high wind or white-out, it might be more prudent to walk.

The return follows the ascent route. The skiing is very easy with wide open spaces down which to chose one's own run. Only in bad visibility are there any problems, for on the featureless hillside it is all too easy to ski off course. In such conditions it would be best to follow one's uphill tracks, and navigation is thus greatly simplified.

Beinn Dorain from the south   W.R. Morrison

The four high mountains to the east and north-east of Bridge of Orchy form a long curving ridge whose western slopes drop in great concave sweeps to Loch Tulla and the headwaters of the River Orchy. This range forms the western bastion of the Breadalbane mountains, and from its summit ridges the mountaineer looks out across the Moor of Rannoch to the Black Mount and the Lochaber peaks. The traverse of these high ridges gives fine skiing of no great difficulty. Although it would be quite possible for a fit party to do all four peaks in one long day, starting at Bridge of Orchy with a car placed at Achallader farm for the return, two shorter days will be described which can be linked together.

Beinn Dorain; 1076m; (OS Sheet 50; 326378).
Beinn an Dothaidh; 1002m; (OS Sheet 50; 332408).
Starting point at Bridge of Orchy station (301395); altitude 160m. Distance 12km. Height climbed 1150m. Time 5-6 hours. Rating: ★★★/III.

Approaching by the main A82 road from the south, Beinn Dorain presents an imposing peak flanked by long steep slopes which do not usually hold good snow on the west side. To its north, Beinn an Dothaidh also has uniformly steep slopes round its western perimeter above Loch Tulla. Between them, however, Coire an Dothaidh gives relatively easy access to the upper parts of both mountains where there is a lot of good skiing and a selection of short to medium length tours which may be extended to Beinn Achaladair (see p39).

Starting from the car park at Bridge of Orchy station, go through the tunnel under the railway onto the moor and ascend on the S side of the Allt Coire an Dothaidh. Towards the head of the corrie, about 50m below the col at its head, there is a small broken cliff with a shelf above it. The easiest route on skis keeps towards the left (N) under the steep and usually ice-covered crags on the Beinn an Dothaidh side of the corrie until it is possible to turn right and make a rising traverse SE up to and along the shelf towards the col.

Before reaching the col bear S up a broad gully with a line of low cliffs on its E side, and reach the very wide, easy-angled N ridge of Beinn Dorain. Ski up this ridge to a false summit, then descend S, dropping 20m and continuing along a narrower ridge with steep slopes on both sides for about 200 metres to the true summit, which in clear weather is a superb viewpoint.

The descent may follow the ascent route on the N ridge all the way back to the col. However, it may be better, after returning past the false summit, to take a line further E, skiing down the shallow corrie at the head of the Allt Coire a'Ghabhalach. This corrie holds snow well and gives a good run, but do not ski too far down before traversing left to reach the col.

Beinn an Dothaidh is well protected by crags and steep ground on most sides, but the ascent from the col is easy. Climb NE on a rising traverse above the crags overlooking Coire a'Ghabhalach to reach less steep slopes as the summit is approached. The present edition of OS Sheet 50 is incorrect in showing two tops; there are three, the middle one being the highest. The drops between these tops along the summit plateau are very small, and at the N edge cornices overhang the cliffs of the NE corrie. Great care is needed skiing along this plateau in bad visibility.

The simplest return to the col is by way of the ascent route, or (if one is skiing off the West Top) down the shallow basin slightly further W. From the cairn at the col ski down onto the shelf 30m below, passing to the right of twin pointed boulders (which are above the small cliff mentioned above), and continue NW on a downward traverse below the big ice-covered crag. Once the slopes below are clear, turn downhill and ski steeply down to easier ground by the Allt Coire an Dothaidh. Easy skiing along the S side of this stream leads back to the station at Bridge of Orchy.

This tour can be extended north-eastwards from Beinn an Dothaidh by skiing SE from the summit, then E down the ridge leading to the bealach at the head of Coire Achaladair. There the traverse of Beinn Achaladair and Beinn a' Chreachain, described on p39, is joined and if it is followed over these two mountains to its end at Achallader farm one gets a superb long 5-star tour. A good trip for fit young skiers on a fine day.

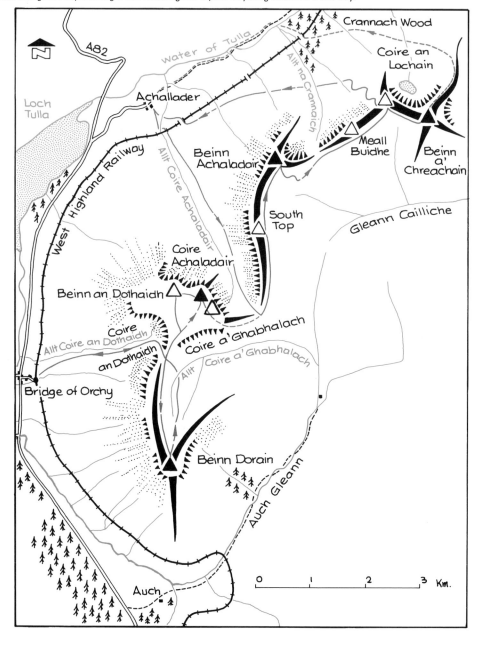

On the ascent to Meall Buidhe, looking towards Beinn Achaladair   D.J. Bennet

Beinn Achaladair; 1039m; (OS Sheet 50; 345434).
Beinn a' Chreachain; 1081m; (OS Sheet 50; 373441).
Starting point at Achallader farm (322443) 1km east of the A82 road near the head of Loch Tulla;
altitude 180m. Distance 16km. Height climbed 1300m. Time 7-8 hours. Rating: ★★★/IV.

The traverse of these two fine mountains starts and finishes at Achallader farm, 1km E of the head of Loch Tulla. At the time of writing there appears to be no objection made to driving along the private road from the A82 towards the farm and parking near the first cottage. From there follow a track S to cross the West Highland Railway and reach the hillside on the E of the Allt Coire Achaladair. The simplest route of ascent, although not the most direct, is right up the corrie to the col at its head, keeping on the E side of the stream. Any attempt to climb directly SE from the railway to the lowest point of the summit ridge of Beinn Achaladair between its two tops is not recommended, even in good snow conditions, for the slope is long and steep. If the snow is soft, there might be a distinct avalanche risk.

Once on the col at the head of Coire Achaladair turn NE then N along a broad, easy-angled ridge to the South Top (1002m) of Beinn Achaladair. It is not worth taking off skins for the short descent along the ridge that precedes the final climb to the summit which is close to the N edge of the mountain, overlooking a long steep drop to the railway far below.

On the descent to the next col which links Beinn Achaladair to Meall Buidhe do not ski along the ridge as it becomes steep and rocky lower down and may be corniced on its precipitous N side. Instead, ski SE from the cairn down easy open slopes, dropping about 150m, then turn NE and make a descending traverse below the rocky flank of the ridge and above a fence which leads NE to the col at 800m.

Continue NE up to the broad level ridge of Meall Buidhe (977m) and traverse its 1km long flat crest. Then descend E slightly to reach the foot of the final climb of 170m to Beinn a' Chreachain. Surprisingly, the exposed and windswept character of these highest stony slopes may result in their having a poorer snow cover than the lower hillsides and corries.

One possible descent route from Beinn a' Chreachain is down the NE ridge for 1km before turning NW towards Crannach Wood. The crest of this ridge is very narrow at one point, and it should be skied with great caution. However, with a good snow cover this is a perfectly feasible route, although there is a long walk back to Achallader farm from Crannach Wood if there is not enough snow low down for skiing.

It is probably better to return to the cairn at the NE end of the level summit ridge of Meall Buidhe. Go about 150 metres SW from this cairn along the level ridge, and then turn right and ski steeply down the NW face of Meall Buidhe. The upper part of the slope is the steepest, and if it is icy or avalanche prone the descent should be undertaken with great care. In good conditions, however, this is an exhilarating ski run. Lower down the angle eases and one should ski W in a long descending traverse high above Crannach Wood. Cross the Allt na Crannaich at about 500m and continue a gradual descent across the lower slopes of Beinn Achaladair to reach the railway and cross it by a bridge near Achallader farm. Do not ski along the railway. If there is complete snow cover, the descent from Meall Buidhe is 4km long, with a drop of 700m.

Stob Ghabhar from Loch Tulla   *D. Scott*

Stob Ghabhar; 1087m; (OS Sheets 41 and 50; 230455).
Creise; 1100m; (OS Sheets 41 and 50; 238507).
Meall a' Bhuiridh; 1108m; (OS Sheets 41 and 50; 251503).
Starting point at Victoria Bridge at the west end of Loch Tulla (271421); altitude 170m. Distance 17km. Height climbed 1570m. Time 7-8 hours. Rating: ★★★★/IV.

These splendid mountains dominate the west side of Rannoch Moor and, when well covered in snow, give one of the best ski tours in Scotland which is also a magnificent mountaineering expedition. It should only be tackled by a strong party with mountaineering experience, equipped with crampons and ice axes. The most difficult section of the traverse is the steep slope from the ridge south of Creise down to the col WSW of Meall a' Bhuiridh. The broken rocks and considerable exposure on this face do not normally present a major difficulty, but if the snow is hard or icy, the descent of this slope may be quite formidable. As the southern slopes of Stob Ghabhar nearly always hold less snow than the north-east face of Meall a' Bhuiridh, the direction recommended, which gives the best downhill runs, is from south to north. The traverse in the opposite direction, however, has the advantage that one can use the tows of Meall a' Bhuiridh to reach its summit quickly and with little effort. One requirement for this tour, irrespective of which way one goes, is a friendly driver or a second car at the end of the traverse.

Turn off the A82 road at Bridge of Orchy and drive along the A8005 road to a point just S of Victoria Bridge where it is usually possible to park a car. Cross the bridge and turn W following the private road along the N bank of the Linne nam Beathach for 1½km to the little hut beside the Allt Toaig.

At this point it is necessary to decide the best line of ascent to Stob Ghabhar, whose SE face appears as a wide corrie between the E and SE ridges, with a waterfall high between them which is best avoided. Normally the best way is across the moorland on the W side of the Allt Toaig to reach the SE ridge which is followed to the point where it joins the E ridge. Continue up the crest of the SE ridge, keeping well away from its right (NE) edge which is often corniced, for ⅓km to the summit.

From the summit of Stob Ghabhar ski NW for 200 metres, then N down a broad and easy-angled slope across which it is usually possible to schuss for over ½km towards the distant ridge of Aonach Mor. Follow this ridge, which has several undulations, but as the ascents are very short it is unnecessary to put on skins. After a further 1½km, at (224476), descend the NE side of the ridge down a fairly steep but otherwise easy slope towards a broad bealach. The lowest point of this col, the Bealach Fuar-chathaidh, lies a further ⅓km NE beyond a small rocky rise. It is a good stopping place, approximately half way along the traverse.

The hillside NE of the bealach is steep and has several scoops which hold snow well and can be skied down on the N to S traverse. However, going in the other direction it is probably best to carry skis up this section unless the snow cover is good on the slopes to the left, which is slightly less steep. Once on the more level ridge above, the ascent ENE to the summit of Clach Leathad (1098m) is straightforward.

From that summit the route continues N parallel to the steep edge of the eastern corrie. Neither the descent nor the following ascent are steep, and one can avoid putting on skins. Just under 1km N of Clach Leathad, at

Skiing west from Clach Leathad on the north to south traverse of the Black Mount   R.Simpson

Pt. 1068m, the route to Meall a' Bhuiridh descends steeply E down a slope of steep snow and broken rocks. It is necessary to carry skis initially, but if snow conditions are good it may be possible to ski down the lower slopes to the col.

An alternative route is to continue N from Pt.1068 along the level ridge for ½km almost to Creise, which is not named on the 1:50000 OS map. About 100 metres S of the summit of Creise there is seldom a cornice on the E side of the ridge, and with no rocks below it is possible to ski down from that point, but the slope is steep and exposed. After descending 100m make a traverse right, down to the col below Meall a' Bhuiridh.

The ridge from this col to the summit of Meall a' Bhuiridh is quite narrow and may have insufficient snow for an ascent on skis, but it is a straightforward climb. From the summit the top of the upper ski tows is a short distance E, and only slightly lower. Ski down the pistes, which if you have arrived at the summit of Meall a' Bhuiridh late in the day may well be deserted. At the foot of the upper tows bear right past the Scottish Ski Club hut and ski NE down to the flat middle slopes of Coire Pollach. Continue NNE, skiing easily across the plateau well to the E of the stream draining the corrie, and finally ski or walk down the steeper hillside above the moor to the bottom of the chairlift and the car park a short distance below it.

If the traverse is done from N to S, the summit of Meall a' Bhuiridh can be quickly and easily reached using the ski lifts. From there the WSW ridge can be descended on skis if there is good snow cover on the crest. The highlight of the traverse may well be the descent from the ridge 1km WSW of Clach Leathad down a steep gully (Grade IV) to the Bealach Fuar-chathaidh. Finally, if there is good snow cover on the SE side of Stob Ghabhar, there is a 3km long run from the summit to the glen down slopes which are fairly easy, but full of route finding interest.

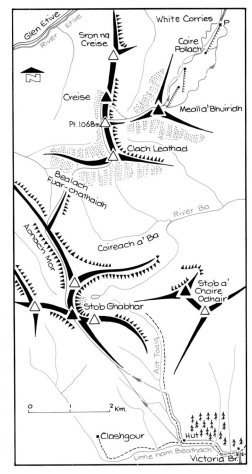

Ben Nevis from Aonach Beag   M.J. Snadden

Ben Nevis; 1344m; (OS Sheet 41; 167713).
Starting point at the distillery (125757) on the A82 road 3km NE of Fort William; altitude 10m.
Distance 16km. Height climbed 1340m. Time 6-8 hours. Alternative starting points at Achintee
(126730) or the youth hostel in Glen Nevis (128718); altitude 30m. Distance 10-12km. Height climbed
1330m. Time 4-6 hours. Rating ★★★★/IV.

Ben Nevis should always be regarded as a serious ski-mountaineering proposition on account of its height, steep
upper slopes, cliff hazard and high mountain snow and weather conditions. If these conditions are good, this is a
fine expedition with superb skiing and views; in bad weather, storm or white-out, Ben Nevis is best avoided, for the
problems of navigation on the summit plateau are considerable and the consequences of errors likely to be very
serious. Completely different snow conditions may be encountered on opposite sides of the mountain, e.g. ice on
the steep SE side above the head of Coire Leis, and loose powder or windslab with avalanche risk at the top of the
Red Burn on the NW side. Ice axe and crampons are essential for this climb, and a rope is also advisable,
particularly if one is making the ascent via Coire Leis.

If there is snow cover down to sea-level, the best route starts at the distillery and follows a path beside the river,
under the railway bridge. Climb near the footpath and private road leading E towards the Allt a' Mhuilinn and reach
open slopes at about 300m. Continue S for 2km to reach Lochan Meall an t-Suidhe, and a few hundred metres to its
SE, at about 600m, intersect the main Ben Nevis footpath which comes up from Glen Nevis.

If skiable snow does not reach down to sea-level, it is better to start at Achintee or the Glen Nevis youth hostel
and carry skis up the Ben Nevis path to Lochan Meall an t-Suidhe.

Above the lochan the skier is faced with an ascent of 600m up the wide and steep NW flank which has a gradient
approaching 30°. At this angle climbing on skis is hard work in any but good conditions. A route zig-zagging
upwards between the line of the path and the Red Burn is best, but keep well clear of crags S of the path. The top of
the Red Burn ends in a shallow scoop which brings the skier onto easier ground, passing ½km S of Carn Dearg and
heading E towards the edge of the cliffs on the NE face of Ben Nevis. Before reaching the edge, which is corniced
and indented by deep gullies, bear SE for about 300 metres and then E for ½km, keeping well away from the cliffs,
to reach the deep indentations of Tower Gully and Gardyloo Gully, then bear NE for 150 metres to the top.

To descend from the summit, ski SW for 150 metres to pass the head of Gardyloo Gully, then W for 500 metres,
then NW towards the head of the Red Burn. (These bearings are crucial. In white-out conditions it is safer to walk,
counting paces). The Red Burn can give fine skiing, but it may be cut up by climbers' footsteps. Ski down the left or
S side initially, then at about 850m, where the burn narrows, cross to the N side and ski NW down to Lochan Meall
an t-Suidhe, thus avoiding very steep convex slopes on the S side of the burn.

For experienced and competent ski-mountaineers there is a superb ascent, starting at the distillery and going up
the Allt a' Mhuilinn past the CIC Hut to Coire Leis. If conditions are good, it may be possible to climb on skis from
the head of the corrie past the abseil posts onto the Carn Mor Dearg Arête, and up the SE shoulder all the way to
the summit. However, it is more likely that one will have to carry skis, and climb this section with ice axe and
crampons. This route is not recommended for the descent.

Looking west from Stob Choire Claurigh to Ben Nevis and the Aonachs   A. Sloan

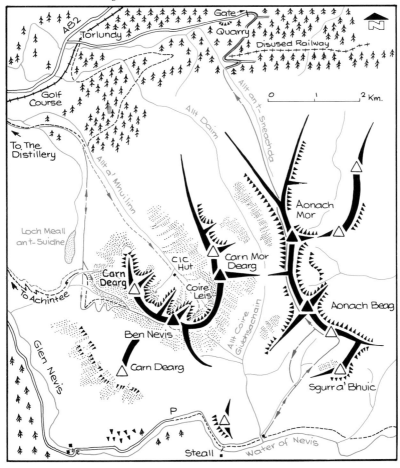

Aonach Beag; 1234m; (OS Sheet 41; 196715).
Aonach Mor; 1221m; (OS Sheet 41; 193730).

Starting point at the car park at the end of the road in Glen Nevis (167691); altitude 160m.

The traverse: Distance 16km. Height climbed 1300m. Time 6-7 hours. Rating: ★★★★/III.

Ascent and return: Distance 22km. Height climbed 1450m. Time 8-9 hours. Rating: ★★★/III.

The traverse of these mountains provides one of the finest tours in the country, but it must be remembered that they are very high and subject to rapid changes of weather. It is also possible to ascend them and then return to the original starting point. Because both mountains have precipitous faces on both E and W sides and because huge cornices form on the edges of the plateaux (particularly on the NE side of the SE ridge of Aonach Beag), good visibility is essential for this tour. An ice-axe and crampons are also necessary.

From the Glen Nevis car park follow the excellent path which has been constructed through the gorge to the W end of the Steall meadows. As the altitude here is only 230m, snow seldom lies for long and it is normally necessary to walk along the 1½km to the ruins at Upper Steall.

Sgurr a'Bhuic is the prominent peak to the NE and the route follows the E bank of the stream which issues from the corrie N of the peak. At first the hillside rises

Aonach Mor from Aonach Beag   W. Wallace

steadily but becomes much steeper under the upper slopes of Sgurr a' Bhuic. In rounding the peak, traverse diagonally upwards across the steep slope to gain the much more gentle slopes of the upper corrie. Cross the bed of the corrie and traverse the S facing slope diagonally upwards to the NE to gain the crest of the SE ridge of Aonach Beag. Follow the ridge first W up several steep sections then, where it flattens, turn NW towards the summit dome of Aonach Beag. This is the section of the ridge at which there are often huge cornices so care should be taken to stay well back from the edge. The final 250m ascent to the summit is up broad open slopes which are not excessively steep. The cairn which marks the summit is very small and is usually completely buried under snow in winter.

The col between the two mountains is ½km to the NW. As the slope is convex with cliffs to the N and steep broken ground below to the W, accurate navigation is needed in poor visibility. As the last 30m to the col consists of broken rocks and is exposed, great care is necessary. Skis have to be carried. The ascent to the summit of Aonach Mor is up an easy angled slope to the N and presents no problem.

To return to Glen Nevis the outward route is reversed to Aonach Beag, then descend S keeping to the W of a shallow gully. There are a few small cliffs at around 750m which should be avoided on the W. Below this cross the stream and descend the outward route to the ruins at Upper Steall.

However, the best end to the tour is to continue the traverse N along the plateau of Aonach Mor which is almost level and narrow between the cliffs to E and W. After ¾km descend NNW down the line of the Allt an-t Sneachda which in its upper part usually holds snow until very late in the season. A ski descent of almost 1000m is possible if the snow extends down to the edge of the forest. Just W of the Allt an-t Sneachda, there is a stile over the fence. Below this a path leads down to an adit at the upper end of the private road in the Leanachan Forest. Follow this road down to the cross-roads at (185777) immediately W of which there is a gate across the road which may be locked and therefore a car should be left on its W side.

Stob Choire Claurigh from the west   D.Snadden

Stob Choire Claurigh; 1177m; (OS Sheet 41; 262739)
Stob Coire an Laoigh; 1115m; (OS Sheet 41; 240725)
Starting point at the disused tramway 2km S of Corriechoille farm (255788); Altitude 200m. Distance 22km. Height climbed 1350m. Time 8-9 hours. Rating: ★★★★/III.

The high ridge of the Grey Corries, which includes two Munros and does not fall below 980m, provides a superb, albeit a fairly long, tour. The traverse may be done in either direction but as the NE to SW direction provides excellent views ahead of the steep eastern corries of Aonach Beag and Aonach Mor and the topmost cliffs of Ben Nevis beyond, this is the recommended option.

The only practicable approach is from the N. From Spean Bridge follow the narrow public road on the S side of the River Spean to Corriechoille farm. The road which goes past the farm and continues for a further 2km to the S is private but there appears to be no objection to driving up to the remains of the disused tramway which is marked on the 1:50000 map. Leave the car here and continue up the track which leads SE through the forest towards the Lairig Leacach. In 1½km, at the upper edge of the forest, leave the track and climb the steep hillside for 200m, heading SSW parallel to the edge of the forest. Above this the angle eases slightly but the gradient is continuous for another 400m S to Stob Coire na Gaibhre on the N edge of Coire na Ceannain. Beyond this top there is a short descent and the ridge narrows. Continue climbing SSE following the steep edge of Coire na Ceannain to the E. At 1100m the ridge flattens before rising into a narrow rocky crest where it will be necessary to carry skis. The summit of Stob Choire Claurigh is just beyond this crest.

As the open hillside above the forest may be bare of snow, an alternative route follows the line of the disused tramway SW to a road on the E side of the stream which drains Coire Choimhlidh. Turn S and follow the road ½km to a dam beyond which traverse the hillside above the stream. 1km beyond the dam several streams converge. Above this, even late in the season, the stream beds hold considerable snow. Follow SE up the course of the stream which drains the corrie under the summit of Stob Choire Claurigh. In the inner corrie there is a steep snow ramp from right to left under the summit rocks which is ascended to gain the end of the rocky crest mentioned above.

From the summit the ridge to the SW is broad and easy angled, thus presenting no difficulty provided there is sufficient snow cover. At ½km from the summit there is a col from which it is possible to traverse the S slope to a lower col ½km farther on or alternatively continue along the crest of the ridge, climbing over a minor top, then skiing down to the second col. At this point the ridge rises and narrows and as it is also rocky for a short distance it is necessary to carry skis. Beyond the rocky section it broadens again and turns W to climb over a minor summit (1104m). It then drops 50m before turning SW to climb 60m to the summit of the second Munro, Stob Coire an Laoigh, which is not named on the 1:50000 map.

Stob Coire Easain, the next top, lies ½km WNW. The descent to the col is 90m and both this descent and the following ascent of 65m are on boulder covered slopes which require a good covering of snow before they are skiable. On a fine day the view from here of the eastern corries of Aonach Mor and Aonach Beag is most impressive.

The descent from Stob Coire Easain into the head of Coire Choimhlidh   G. Mackenzie

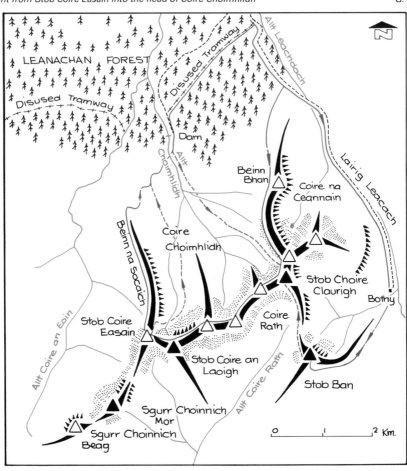

Stob Ban from the north   *D. Scott*

When there is good snow cover, the N ridge over Beinn na Socaich provides the fastest descent, keeping to the W side of the crest (the E side is precipitous). Ski easily along this broad ridge for 2km, then turn NNE down open slopes heading NE for the point where the Allt Choimhlidh flows into the forest. Very little snow is required to make this last part of the descent skiable as there is an almost complete absence of boulders on the grassy slopes.

If there is a lack of snow on the crest of the ridge, an alternative descent is to leave it ⅓km NNE of Stob Coire Easain and ski steeply down into the corrie to the E which holds snow until late in the season. Continue down the corrie for 1½km to 650m where it becomes fairly level and the stream drops to the NE. At that point leave the stream and bear NNW on a gradually descending traverse round the base of Beinn na Socaich to join the descent route described above.

Before reaching the forest, cross the Allt Choimhlidh to its E side and reach the end of the road at the dam just below the tree-line. Finally there is a long slog, probably on foot, down the road for ½km and then along the line of the disused tramway back to the day's starting point.

Stob Ban; 977m; (OS Sheet 41; 266724).
Starting point as for the preceding tour. Distance 17km. Height climbed 850m. Time 6-7 hours.
Rating: ★★★/III.

This is a remote little peak lying hidden behind the high ridge of the Grey Corries. The ascent of Stob Ban on skis should only be made if there is a good snow cover low down for there is a long approach to the peak, and if there is not a good snow cover then skis may have to be carried for a long way. From the starting point at the disused tramway follow the broad road into the forest. Beyond the forest continue along a narrower track for 5km to cross the highest point of the Lairig Leacach and descend 1½km to a small, but habitable bothy from which there is a good view of Stob Ban.

Just beyond the bothy cross a burn to the point where the path divides. Take the right fork and after 100 metres bear SW up the hillside. The broad lower slopes gradually narrow to a ridge which at 750m levels to a flat shoulder below the final steep and rocky rise to the summit. The direct ascent of the final 150m of the E ridge involves a climb with crampons and ice-axe, carrying skis. It may be possible to avoid this direct ascent by a rising traverse across the S side of the final peak to reach the SW ridge, which is less steep, not far below the summit.

The simplest way back is to retrace the outward route. A much more interesting way, which adds 380m of ascent, is to descend steeply NW down a bouldery slope (possibly carrying skis) to reach a wide col at 800m. From there ski N up the steep but broad ridge of Stob Choire Claurigh to the point where it levels out, and turn NW to reach the summit a short distance further. The descent is best made down the long N ridge of Stob Choire Claurigh to Stob Coire na Gaibhre then down the easy slopes of Beinn Bhan to the forest, and finally along the road through the forest to the starting point.

Beinn a' Chaorainn from the south-east   *D.J. Bennet*

Beinn Teallach; 915m; (OS Sheet 41; 361860).
Beinn a' Chaorainn; 1052m; (OS Sheet 41; 386851).
Starting point 11km E of Roy Bridge on the A86 road at Roughburn cottages, (377814); altitude 270m.
Distance 14km. Height climbed 1100m. Time 5-6 hours. Rating: ★★★/III.

These two mountains give a very pleasant tour which begins with an ascent of the easy southern slopes of Beinn Teallach, continues along the ridge above the east corries of Beinn a' Chaorainn and ends with a grand run down Coire Clachaig.

Starting from the A86 road just E of Roughburn, follow the forest road NW for 1km, turn left and continue W, leaving the forest and crossing flat grassland to the Allt a' Chaorainn. The crossing of this burn is best made low down, although if it is frozen or snow-covered there is no problem in crossing higher up. Climb N along the W side of the burn to the NE corner of Upper Laggan Wood, and continue up the broad easy slopes of Beinn Teallach.

From the summit ski N initially down Coire Dubh Sguadaig, then curve round E to reach flat ground at 620m just N of the cairn at the head of the Allt a' Chaorainn (372868). With a good snow cover there is a more direct and very scenic route down through the crags of the NE face (Tom Mor) which is not particularly difficult.

Ski up the NW shoulder of Beinn a' Chaorainn to the N Top (1045m), and follow the ridge S at a safe distance from the corniced E edge to the main summit. Continue to the S Top (1050m) from which there are two possible descents. The steeper and more direct route goes down Coire Clachaig and leads to a gate in the forest fence at the boundary between old and new plantations above Roughburn. Continue down the clearing between these plantations to the forest road, and depending on snow cover either ski down this road to the starting point, or go straight down through the forest beside the fence. The alternative route from the S Top goes down the SW ridge, passing to the NW of Meall Clachaig to reach the gate at the W edge of the forest.

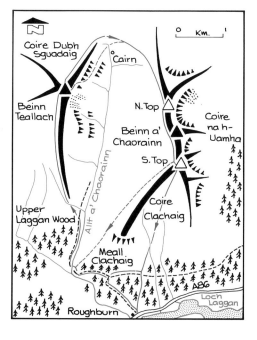

Stob a' Choire Mheadhoin from the north-east   *W.R. Morrison*

Stob a' Choire Mheadhoin; 1106m; (OS Sheet 41; 316736).
Stob Coire Easain; 1116m; (OS Sheet 41; 308730).
Starting point on the minor road from the A86 7km E of Roy Bridge to Fersit near the N end of An Dubh Lochan (349790); altitude 240m. For Stob a' Choire Mheadhoin only: Distance 14km. Height climbed 870m. Time 4-5 hours. Including Stob Coire Easain: Distance 16km. Height climbed 1170m. Time 5-6 hours. Rating: ★★★/III (IV to Stob Coire Easain).

These two mountains, known as the Easains, are particularly fine, with steep slopes overlooking Loch Treig, the Lairig Leacach and the head of Coire Laire. However, the north-east ridge of Stob a' Choire Mheadhoin gives an easy ascent with a choice of descent routes on its NW flank. In high winds progress up the exposed upper ridge can be arduous, especially if the steep final slopes are icy.

From the starting point go SW across the outflow of An Dubh Lochan to reach the line of an old railway track at a rock cutting. Follow the track NW towards Coire Laire for a short distance, then climb SW up easy slopes onto the ridge above the plantation on the SE side of Coire Laire. Traverse below the crags on the NW side of Meall Cian Dearg and gain the ridge above at about 800m. (An alternative route to this point is along the old railway track for 2km to the SW corner of the plantation, followed by a steeper climb S to reach the ridge). Continue up the ridge to the summit of Stob a' Choire Mheadhoin.

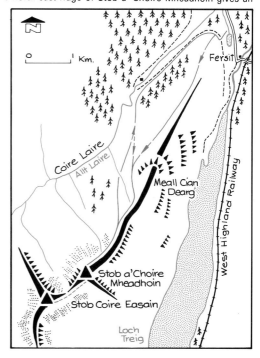

The ridge leading SW to the col at 970m and up to Stob Coire Easain is very steep, and should only be skied if the snow conditions are excellent, which is not often the case. It may be better, if one wants to climb this peak, to go on foot with ice axe and crampons.

Returning from Stob a' Choire Mheadhoin, ski down the crest of the ridge for at least ½km to get a choice of runs N down to Coire Laire, or down the ridge itself. If skiing down into Coire Laire, make a long descending traverse above the open birchwoods on the hillside to reach the railway track which has a good surface and a very easy gradient back to the starting point.

Beinn a' Chlachair from Loch Pattack   *D.J. Bennet*

Creag Pitridh; 924m; (OS Sheet 42; 488814).
Geal Charn; 1049m; (OS Sheet 42; 504812).
Beinn a' Chlachair; 1088m; (OS Sheet 42; 471781).
Starting point on the A86 road in Glen Spean 1km WSW of Moy Lodge at (433830); altitude 250m.
Distance 21km. Height climbed 1280m. Time 7-8 hours. Rating: ★★★★/IV.

These three peaks, located to the south of Loch Laggan, make a fine ski tour over interesting and varied terrain. All the summits are boulder strewn, and need a generous snow cover for good skiing. One would be well advised to carry ice-axe, crampons and harscheisen on this tour.

The traverse is probably best undertaken in a clockwise direction as the descent from Beinn a' Chlachair gives an excellent finish to the day. Cross the concrete bridge from the starting point and follow the private estate road on the E bank of the Abhainn Ghuilbinn for 1km, then turn E, still following the road to reach another track which leads round the base of Binnein Shuas to Lochan na h-Earba.

On reaching the SW end of this loch leave the track and ascend SE following the line of the Allt Coire Pitridh up fairly easy slopes below Sgurr an t-Saighdeir. At 550m turn NE and make as direct a line as possible, zig-zagging between small rocky outcrops, to the pointed summit of Creag Pitridh which gives good views NW to Binnein Shuas and Creag Meagaidh. Descend to the col separating Creag Pitridh from Geal Charn by skiing S at first, avoiding rock outcrops by keeping to their right (W) and then curving E down the col. The flat summit of Geal Charn is easily reached by skinning up straightforward slopes E from the col.

The run from Geal Charn gives almost 300m of skiing down to the pass W of Loch a' Bhealaich Leamhain, the best line being down the W flank of the SW ridge. The ascent from the pass to the flat NE ridge of Beinn a' Chlachair can be difficult on skis as the slope is steep, rocky and often icy. On the writer's ascent the steepest slopes were negotiated by sidestepping upwards, using harscheisen. This technique can give a sensation of insecurity similar to that experienced while slab climbing. Some might prefer to carry skis and use crampons for this section, or make a rising traverse lower down to gain easier slopes near the E side of Coire Mor a' Chlachair.

Having reached the broad NE ridge, continue easily along it and turn W above the lip of Coire Mor a' Chlachair to reach the large summit cairn, not far from the edge of the corrie.

The run down the open slopes of the NW flank of Beinn a' Chlachair gives 700m of straightforward and enjoyable skiing once having first weaved a way through the boulder strewn slopes just W of the summit cairn. A track is reached near the ruins of Lubvan bothy, and is followed N to meet the outward route just W of the lochan on the Allt Meall Ardruighe.

An alternative descent, which can be inspected on the ascent and may give excellent skiing, is down the NE corrie of Beinn a' Chlachair. From the summit return E then NE round the rim of Coire Mor a'Chlachair and ski NE down a wide unnamed corrie, often well snow filled, and reach the Allt Coire Pitridh where the uphill route is joined.

The approach to Beinn a' Chlachair along the north-east ridge   *D.J. Bennet*

Beinn a' Chlachair and Geal Charn can also be approached from the E, starting at Loch Pattack which can be reached by car if permission is obtained to drive along the private road from Dalwhinnie past Ben Alder Lodge to the loch. From the SW corner of the loch follow the track W to the Allt Cam. The crossing of this stream may be difficult or impossible unless the water is low or there is a firm covering of ice. Once on the N side of the stream Beinn a' Chlachair can be reached by climbing W over gradually rising ground to the final short steep slope leading to the NE ridge. Geal Charn is climbed up easy slopes to the E of Loch a' Bhealaich Leamhain.

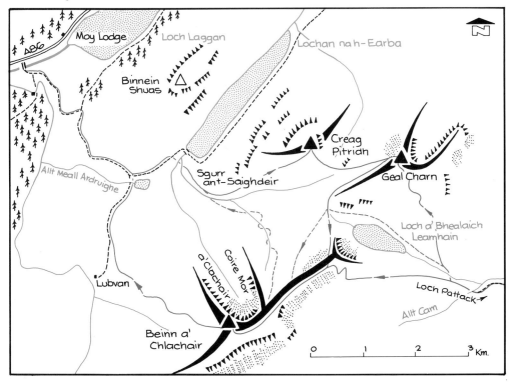

On the ridge from Carn Liath to Stob Poite Coire Ardair looking towards Creag Meagaidh   D.J. Bennet

Carn Liath; 1006m; (OS Sheet 34; 472904),
Stob Poite Coire Ardair; 1053m; (OS Sheets 34 and 42; 418875).
Creag Meagaidh; 1130m; (OS Sheets 34 and 42; 418875).
Starting point near Aberarder farm on the A86 road by Loch Laggan (483873); altitude 250m.
Distance 18km. Height climbed 1150m. Time 7-8 hours. Rating: ★★★★/III.

The Creag Meagaidh group is one of the highest mountain massifs between Lochaber and the Cairngorms, and situated as it is far from the western seaboard it has a good snow-holding record. The traverse of the three Munros and the long horseshoe ridge round Coire Ardair is a fine high level tour, always above 920m, and on a clear day there are splendid views of the great crags of Coire Ardair. For most of its length the ridge is smooth and broad and the skiing easy, with a very fine descent of 700m at the end of the traverse. The most likely problem may be route-finding and navigation in bad visibility, particularly on the vast and featureless plateau of Creag Meagaidh itself.

Starting from the A86 road at Aberarder farm, climb N up the steepening slopes of Carn Liath to a brief level section of the broad S ridge of this hill. Continue up smooth featureless slopes with intermittent fence posts leading to the summit, a large cairn on the flat plateau.

Ski W along the broad smooth ridge, descending slightly to a well-defined little col at 920m. The next climb to Meall an t-Snaim (969m) and the need to put on skins can be avoided by traversing horizontally along the S flank of the ridge, and descending slightly to reach the next col which forms a very narrow notch in the otherwise level ridge. (In bad visibility or icy conditions it might be better to stay on the crest rather than traverse below it as described above). From the notch a short steep climb leads back onto the broad crest, over Sron Coire a' Chriochairein (991m) and round the corniced edge of Coire a' Chriochairein, following a line of fence posts which continues over another indistinct Top (1051m) to the summit of Stob Poite Coire Ardair.

Ski WSW down a broad easy ridge for about 400 metres, then turn S and descend more steeply to The Window, the narrow pass at the head of Coire Ardair. (In bad visibility beware not to turn S too soon after leaving Stob Poite Coire Ardair, as there are steep crags NE of The Window). At this point the traverse can be shortened by skiing E through the pass and descending Coire Ardair, but after the initial steep run down to the lochan there is a long gradual descent for 5km back to Aberarder.

Continuing the traverse to Creag Meagaidh, climb SE from The Window up a steep slope with the crags of Coire Ardair far to one's left. Then as the plateau is reached, bear S then WSW past one cairn to reach the summit of Creag Meagaidh at another large cairn.

Return due E for 1½km to a wide col and climb slightly over the broad hump of Puist Coire Ardair (1070m) to reach the narrower ridge beyond. This section of the route requires very careful navigation in bad visibility as the plateau is quite featureless, and there are precipitous corries to the N and S. There are a few fence posts E of Puist

Leaving the summit of Creag Meagaidh at sundown   *D.J. Bennet*

Coire Ardair to help navigation. Continue E, skiing more steeply down to the level ridge of Sron a' Choire (1001m). It is not necessary to climb to this Top, but a slightly descending traverse ENE leads to a small cairn on its SE shoulder. From there a very fine run goes down the shallow east-facing corrie of the Sron. This is a vast concave bowl which holds snow well and gives excellent skiing down to the level moor on the SW side of the Allt Coire Ardair. Continue down this side of the stream almost to Aberarder and cross by a footbridge a few hundred metres W of the farm.

From the summit of Creag Meagaidh another good and quicker descent route is down the Moy Burn, but it leads to the A86 road several kilometres SW of Aberarder. The slopes immediately S of the Creag Meagaidh cairn are steep, and the safest route goes SE at first before turning SW towards the head of the Burn. This may be preferred as a quicker way off the mountain in bad weather or approaching darkness.

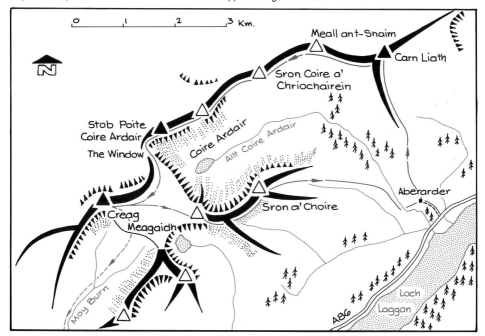

Chno Dearg from Stob Coire Sgriodain   *W.R. Morrison*

Stob Coire Sgriodain; 976m; (OS Sheet 41; 356744).
Chno Dearg; 1047m; (OS Sheet 41; 377741).
Starting point at the end of the public road off the A86 in Glen Spean to Fersit (351783); altitude 240m. Distance 13km. Height climbed 940m. Time 4-5 hours. Rating: ★★/II.

The circuit of these two mountains, possibly with Meall Garbh included, gives a fairly easy but satisfying tour with good terrain for downhill skiing. The big open corrie enclosed by these mountains holds snow well, and is sheltered from the worst of the westerly weather by the Grey Corries.

From the end of the public road at Fersit go E along the private road over two bridges to reach open moorland 200 metres beyond the last house. Leave the road near a shed and ascend easy slopes SSE, following close to the Allt Chaorach Beag. Above 600m the E face of Sron na Garbh-bheinne looks rocky and unskiable, and an ascent across the N face towards the W, though feasible, is not recommended. Instead, continue along the stream towards Lochan Coire an Lochain to about 700m (½km N of the lochan), then turn W and climb any one of the broad gullies leading up to the ridge between Sron na Garbh-bheinne and Stob Coire Sgriodain. These gullies are less steep and rocky than they appear at first sight, and they interlink at various points to give many interesting routes. The ridge up to Stob Coire Sgriodain is quite rocky, but adequate snow cover will most likely be found on the E side of the crest.

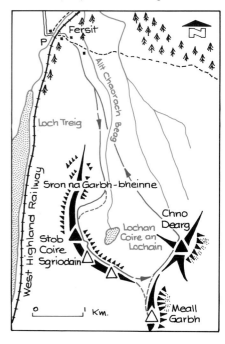

When skiing off the summit of Stob Coire Sgriodain it is probably best to make a brief detour SE, then turn SW to reach the first col. The next section over two minor tops (960m and 925m) is liable to be bouldery, but beyond there is an easy run down to a broad featureless col at 900m. From there Chno Dearg is reached by an easy climb NE to its prominent cairn on a flat summit which, if windswept, may be rather too bouldery for easy skiing. Meall Garbh can be included with little extra effort by climbing SE from the col to the level ridge where the cairn is on the S top.

The best descent from the summit of Chno Dearg is an almost direct line towards Fersit, giving an exceptionally uniform gradient down wide open slopes that hold snow well. With a complete snow cover there is a 4½km run with 750m of descent. With less than complete cover the stream-beds will probably give the best runs, provided they are snow-filled.

Ben Alder (left) and Sgor Gaibhre (centre) from the north-west ridge of Carn Dearg C.R. Ford

Carn Dearg; 941m; (OS Sheets 41 and 42; 418661).
Sgor Gaibhre; 955m; (OS Sheets 41 and 42; 444674).
Starting point at Corrour Station on the West Highland Railway (356664); altitude 410m. Distance 19km. Height climbed 780m. Time 6 hours. Rating: ★★/II.

These two hills of long ridges and wide corries are at the north-east corner of Rannoch Moor, and they are among the few Scottish hills that are more easily reached by train than by car. The West Highland Railway between Rannoch and Corrour stations crosses the desolate moorland at the foot of Carn Dearg, and the traverse of the two hills from one station to the other is a good expedition. The pleasure of this tour depends greatly on the conditions, for the hills are undistinguished and there is a lot of very easy-angled skiing. Snow cover down to the moor is essential. On a clear day the views alone are adequate reward, and on good snow you will enjoy miles of easy ski-running. On a dull day with wet snow, however, there may be a lot of hard poling along the long glen of the Allt Eigheach on the return to Rannoch Station.

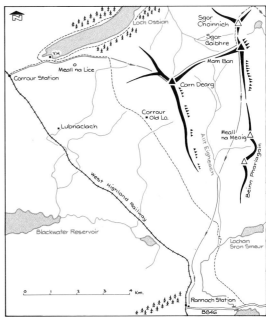

Access to Corrour is by the early morning train from Glasgow to Fort William, and the time available for the tour depends on when the afternoon train passes through Rannoch Station.

From Corrour ski along the track to the head of Loch Ossian, losing a few metres of height. Leave the track near the youth hostel and make a rising traverse along the path round the N side of Meall na Lice for 2km. Continue E up a wide open corrie to gain the NW ridge of Carn Dearg. This broad ridge provides a gradual ascent of 1½km to the summit of Carn Dearg. The view W to Ben Nevis and the Mamores is superb. Turn NE and ski down a broad easy ridge to the Mam Ban col, then climb a steeper ridge to the summit of Sgor Gaibhre.

The return to Rannoch Station is 9km, with a drop of 660m. Ski down the S ridge of Sgor Gaibhre for 2km, then make a long, very gradual descending traverse across the W flank of Meall na Meoig and Beinn Pharlagain for 3km to reach the Allt Eigheach. Cross to the W of the stream and, keeping to high ground, reach the railway 1½km N of Rannoch Station.

From the summit of Sgor Gaibhre the traverse may be continued N then E to Benalder Cottage as the first day of a splendid two day traverse from Corrour to Dalwhinnie over Ben Alder. From Sgor Gaibhre ski down the steep NW flank, then N to the Bealach nan Sgor and ascend 230m to Sgor Choinnich. Avoid the steep E face and ski N then NE to Carn a' Bhealaich at 750m.

From there descend SE down a steep slope to the corrie N of Lochan a' Bhealaich from where an easy run of 5km down the Allt Tom a' Chogaidh leads to Benalder Cottage, where the footbridge over the Alder Burn shown on the 1:50000 map has been washed away by a flood.

Distance 16km. Height climbed 910m. Time 5-6 hours. Rating: ★★★/III.

Beinn Bheoil and Ben Alder from Loch Pattack   D.J. Bennet

Ben Alder; 1148m; (OS Sheet 42; 496718).
Beinn Bheoil; 1019m; (OS Sheet 42; 517717).
Starting point at the shed near Loch Pattack (548787), altitude 440m, or at Culra Bothy (523762), altitude 460m, both accessible from Dalwhinnie by the private road along the north-west side of Loch Ericht to Ben Alder Lodge and Loch Pattack. From Culra, distance 18km. Height climbed 970m. Time 6-7 hours. Add 8km and 2 hours if starting from the shed near Loch Pattack. Rating: ★★★★/IV.

Lying between Loch Ericht to the east and the Geal-Charn group to the west, Ben Alder, with its lower neighbour Beinn Bheoil, occupies a central position in the Highlands, midway between the Lochaber mountains and the Cairngorms. It is a huge flat-topped mountain, very prominent in views from the SW across Rannoch Moor and from Dalwhinnie to the NE, its great high plateau dominating the surrounding mountains and its corries holding snow until early summer.

The approaches to Ben Alder include the route from Dalwhinnie to Loch Pattack and Culra Bothy, and this is probably the best choice. Another good starting point for the ascent is Benalder Cottage 4km S of the summit, reached either from Corrour Station over Carn Dearg and Sgor Gaibhre as described above, or from the W end of Loch Rannoch by the track to the S end of Loch Ericht. All these approaches are very long, and emphasise the remoteness of Ben Alder.

The entire northern perimeter of Ben Alder, from the Bealach Dubh right round to the Bealach Breabag, is a continuous line of steep crags, rocky ridges and corries, and the ski-mountaineer approaching from Culra must outflank these obstacles to the S unless he is prepared to shoulder his skis and do some serious climbing. The easiest way from Culra to Ben Alder is SW up the Allt a' Bhealaich Dhuibh to the Bealach Dubh, a splendid pass, then SW round the W side of the knoll Meall an t-Slugain and S to reach the broad W shoulder which is climbed due E to the summit.

An alternative and very interesting route of distinctly Alpine character is the Long Leachas ridge which drops from the summit plateau directly towards Culra. It should be possible to ski up to about 800m at the foot of the narrow rocky section of the ridge, then carrying skis on the rucksack and with crampons on, scramble up the ridge which is quite narrow and exposed in places. It should not be attempted on a windy day! At 1000m the ridge ends on the summit plateau and the top is 1½km distant to the SSW.

From the summit ski SSW for ½km, then SE, keeping well clear of the edge of the Garbh Choire which often has very large cornices. Continue SE down the steep slope above the Bealach Breabag, taking care to avoid the crags on the northern part of this slope. Aim to ski down near the stream shown on the 1981 OS 1:50000 map just S of these crags at (504704). (The 1976 OS 1:50000 First Series map does not show this slope correctly).

At the Bealach Breabag one joins the route from Benalder Cottage which goes directly up the corrie N of the cottage to the bealach, and may be continued to Ben Alder by ascending the descent route just described.

From the bealach it is possible to make a direct return to Culra by skiing N past Loch a' Bhealaich Bheithe, either by its W or E shore, and across the lower moor to Culra and Loch Pattack.

To complete the traverse over Beinn Bheoil, climb the easy slope NE from the Bealach Breabag to Sron Coire na h-Iolaire (955m). From this top go NW briefly round the edge of the corrie and reach the long ridge leading to Beinn Bheoil. This ridge is quite easy, but does not always hold snow well. From the summit of Beinn Bheoil continue N along the broad ridge for 2km to a level shoulder at 900m, and on down the best snow, either on the ridge or its W flank, to pleasant slopes leading down to Culra.

Looking north-east from the Bealach Dubh
R. Ferguson

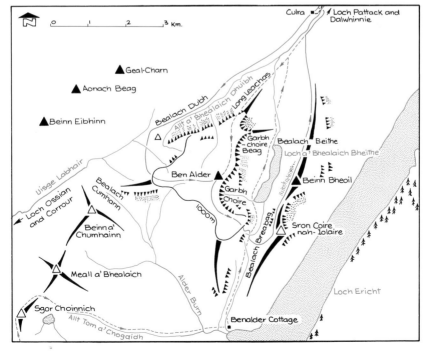

Geal-Charn, Aonach Beag and Beinn Eibhinn from Glen Spean   *D.J. Bennet*

Carn Dearg; 1034m; (OS Sheet 42; 504764).
Geal-Charn; 1132m; (OS Sheet 42; 471745).
Aonach Beag; 1114m; (OS Sheet 42; 458742).
Beinn Eibhinn; 1100m; (OS Sheet 42; 449733).
Starting point at the shed near Loch Pattack (548787), altitude 440m, or at Culra Bothy (523762), altitude 460m, both accessible from Dalwhinnie by the private road along the north-west side of Loch Ericht to Ben Alder Lodge and Loch Pattack. From Culra, distance 23km. Height climbed 1270m. Time 8-9 hours. Add 8km and 2 hours if starting from the shed near Loch Pattack. Rating: ★★★★★/IV.

This great range of mountains, 9km long, lies to the N of the Ben Alder group in the heart of the Central Highlands, remote from all public roads. Because of their height and distance from the coast, these mountains hold snow well, they have some splendid ridges which are narrow and steep enough to give demanding skiing, and great corries which are often snow-filled until late spring. These features, added to the inaccessibility and character of the mountains makes their traverse on skis one of the best expeditions of its kind in Scotland.

Points of access to these mountains include Dalwhinnie to the NE, Moy on the A86 road in Glen Spean and Laggan Bridge to the N, and Corrour Station on the West Highland Railway to the SW. The classic traverse, which only really fit skiers should contemplate, is from Corrour Station to Dalwhinnie, or vice versa, a two day expedition. For most ski-mountaineers a starting point near the range is desirable, and Culra Bothy 15km SW of Dalwhinnie is the ideal base. It may be possible to get permission to drive along the private road from Dalwhinnie Station to the shed near Loch Pattack, from where it is a 4km walk to Culra.

It is advisable to reserve this tour for late winter or spring when the snow on the steeper slopes should be consolidated, and the road to Loch Pattack is not likely to be blocked by snow. Long daylight hours are also necessary if an early morning start in darkness is to be avoided.

Starting from Culra, the ascent of Carn Dearg is very easy by the NE shoulder, as is the long NE ridge rising from Loch Pattack. From the summit ski WSW down a broad ridge and over the rise of Diollaid a' Chairn (922m) to the narrowing ridge leading to the col below Geal-Charn. The arête from the col up to the plateau of Geal-Charn is steep and rocky, and it is probably better to climb it on foot, carrying skis, rather than attempt a circuitous route on skis to the N or S. Once the plateau has been reached, ski WSW for 1km to the flat summit of Geal-Charn which overlooks Coire na Coichille.

Descend in the same direction down the ridge towards Aonach Beag. The N side is steep and corniced, but the crest is broad enough for skiing. The ascent to Aonach Beag is quite steep, and it may be easier to ascend on foot if conditions are icy. The continuation of the ridge SW from Aonach Beag to the col and the ascent to Beinn Eibhinn is more difficult than anything encountered so far; there are steep drops on both side of the narrow ridge and a good covering of spring snow is desirable.

The return from Beinn Eibhinn to Culra poses some questions as to the best route. One might ski more or less due E down steep slopes to the head of the Uisge Labhair, and then cross the Bealach Dubh to return to Culra, but unless there is a good snow cover low down, this will involve a long walk carrying skis.

In good weather and time permitting, it is undoubtedly better to return over Aonach Beag and Geal-Charn. From that summit ski E across the plateau for 1km then SE down a short steep slope to the col W of Sgor Iutharn. From there a superb run can be had down the steep but fairly open gully to Loch an Sgoir (clearly indicated as a stream on the OS 1:50000 map). This run has all the character and challenge that is the best of ski-mountaineering and gives its greatest rewards, the joys of adventurous skiing in remote corries. From the loch one can either make a descending traverse across the S face of Carn Dearg to reach Culra, or continue downhill to the Allt a' Bhealaich Dhuibh and so to Culra along the stream.

At the col between Geal-Charn and Carn Dearg   *W.R. Morrison*

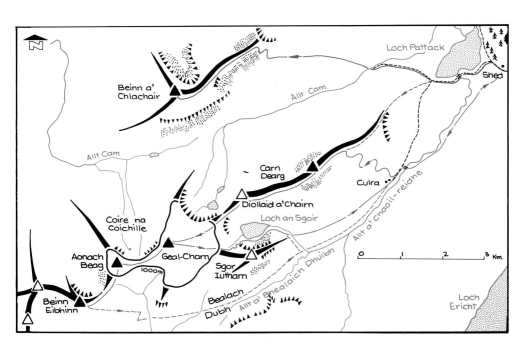

Skiing along the edge of the east corrie of A'Chailleach   *D.J. Bennet*

A'Chailleach; 930m; (OS Sheet 35; 681042).
Carn Sgulain; 920m; (OS Sheet 35; 684059).
Carn Dearg; 945m; (OS Sheet 35; 635024).
Starting point at the end of the public road from Newtonmore up Glen Banchor near the foot of the Allt a' Chaorainn (692997); altitude 300m. Distance 23km. Height climbed 980m. Time 7-8 hours. Rating: ★★★/II.

The wide undulating plateau of the Monadh Liath north-west of Newtonmore gives an interesting, yet not too demanding ski tour taking in three Munros with very little loss of height between their summits. A line of fence posts aids navigation for a long section of the tour across the plateau. Nordic skis are a distinct advantage on this traverse as the undulating nature of the plateau makes attaching and then detaching skins from Alpine skis rather tiresome, and all the climbs and descents (with the exception of the first part of the run down from Carn Dearg) are quite gradual.

From the end of the public road in Glen Banchor follow the track N up the E bank of the Allt a' Chaorainn. After 2km cross the burn and ascend NW past a small bothy to the ridge between Geal Charn and A'Chailleach. From the col climb NE to gain the first Munro, A'Chailleach, which has a big corrie just E of the large summit cairn.

To minimise the loss of height on the next part of the traverse, ski W for ½km to the head of the Allt Cuil na Caillich before ascending NNE to meet the line of fence posts which is followed E to reach the summit of Carn Sgulain. (A warning may be given about skiing more directly from A'Chailleach to Carn Sgulain. The Allt Cuil na Caillich, which has to be crossed, flows in quite a steep-sided gully, whose N bank is often corniced).

Route finding from Carn Sgulain to Carn Ban is made easy by following a line of fence posts for 6km across the plateau. Four minor summits are encountered on the way, but the height never falls below 850m. The distinctive pointed summit of Carn Dearg lies 1km SSE of Carn Ban and is easily reached from the col between them, keeping a safe distance away from the edge of the E corrie.

The descent involves returning a few hundred metres NNW to the col between Carn Dearg and Carn Ban and then skiing NE above a line of rock outcrops down relatively steep slopes to the head of Gleann Ballach. Continue down the glen on the NE side of the Allt Ballach for 1½km and then bear E across the flat ground between Meall na Ceardaich and Creag Liath. The Allt Fionndrigh (which has steep banks in places) should be crossed by a footbridge at (659019) to reach the track on its NE side. Ski down this track to reach Glen Banchor at a point just E of Glen Banchor farm, and follow the main track in the glen back to the starting point.

Two other shorter ski tours, both suitable for Nordic skis, can be made on the slightly lower hills NE of Carn Sgulain. From Kingussie drive up the road on the E side of the Allt Mor to the golf course, and continue on foot or on skis up the private road past Pitmain Lodge. Eventually the track crosses the Allt Mor and climbs across the S flank of Carn an Fhreiceadain (878m), and this hill can be ascended from the track up its broad S ridge.

Several kilometres further NE, Geal-charn Mor (824m) and Geal-charn Beag (741m) can be approached by the hill track which leaves the A9 road at Lynwilg, 2km SW of Aviemore. This track climbs to the pass between the two hills, and both can be climbed easily from its highest point.

The approach to Carn Dearg at the head of Gleann Ballach   D.J. Bennet

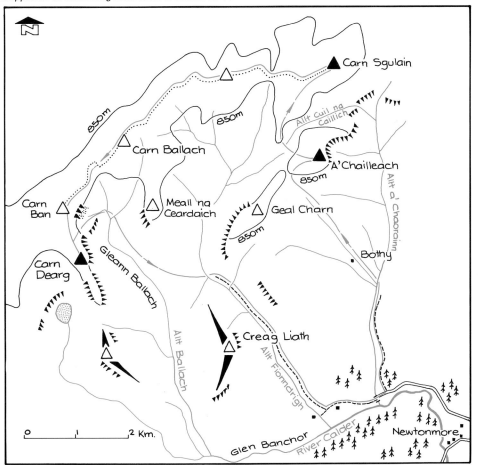

The approach to Glen Charn at the head of the Piper's Burn   D.J. Bennet

Geal Charn; 926m; (OS Sheet 35; 561988).
Starting point at the Spey Dam (582938) 3km west of Laggan Bridge on the A86 road; altitude 280m.
Distance 15km. Height climbed 650m. Time 5 hours. Rating: ★★/II.

This Geal Charn is the western outlier of the Monadh Liath hills, separated from them by Glen Markie. Like the rest of the Monadh Liath, it has a flat featureless summit plateau, but it also has a fine east-facing corrie holding Lochan a' Choire. The rim of this corrie is often impressively corniced in spring, and midway between Geal Charn and its south-east top Beinn Sgiath the headwall is split by a big ice-carved gully, the Uinneag a' Choire Lochan, which might give a challenging ski run. This possibility apart, Geal Charn is a short tour with easy skiing.

From the Spey Dam, where cars may be parked, the first 4km of the approach goes up the track on the E side of the Markie Burn. This is a tedious walk carrying skis if the snow-line is not low enough to permit skiing, so it is worth waiting for such conditions to do this tour. Cross the Markie Burn (no bridge) near the foot of the Piper's Burn and climb NW into the lower part of Choire Lochan. Continue NW, leaving the lochan far to your left, and climb onto the broad ridge on the NE side of the corrie. Once on this ridge ski easily W then SW round the rim of the corrie up to the level plateau, and bear away rightwards to reach the huge summit cairn. In bad visibility a line of fence posts is helpful for finding the cairn. Once the level plateau is reached near the N end of the corrie's steep headwall, these posts are some distance away to the right (W). Bear SW to converge with them, then follow them S to the point where the line of posts suddenly turns E. From there the summit cairn of Geal Charn is about 100 metres W.

The return is best made by the same route, and there is plenty of easy skiing across the plateau, down the corrie and finally, if snow conditions permit, along the track in Glen Markie. Those seeking a more sporting and spectacular descent might care to try the Uinneag a' Choire Lochan, whose top is reached by skiing SE from Geal Charn for ½km. Be warned, however, for the gully is overlooked by steep avalanche-prone slopes and cornices, and it runs straight down to Lochan a' Choire.

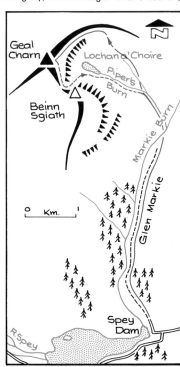

Meall Chuaich and Carn na Caim from the cairns of Geal-charn   *D.J. Bennet*

A'Bhuidheanach Bheag; 936m; (OS Sheet 42; 661776).
Carn na Caim; 941m; (OS Sheet 42; 677822).
Starting point ⅓km north of the summit of Drumochter Pass on the A9 road (631763); altitude 460m.
Distance 13km. Height climbed 700m. Time 4-5 hours. Rating: ★★/II.

One of the attractions of these hills is that they are easily accessible from the A9 road, and if two cars are used a relatively short traverse can be completed in a short mid-winter day. In addition, their plateaux are grassy and can be skied under a thin cover of snow. Nordic skis are undoubtedly more suitable for the tops, but some of the descent routes are quite steep and therefore more suited to alpine skis. In poor visibility accurate navigation on the plateau is essential as it is quite featureless and there are several steep-sided gullies cutting into it from the west.

At the starting point there is a lay-by on the E side of the A9 road from which an initial steep ascent of 180m ENE leads to more gentle slopes and a shallow stream bed. This is ascended to reach the plateau near the point where the march fence turns E. This fence is followed E for 1km to the summit cairn of A'Bhuidheanach Bheag, the highest point at the SW end of a vast plateau which stretches away to the NE.

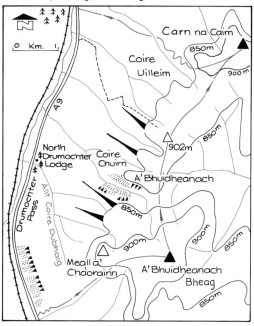

From the summit ski N for 1½km, initially across the flat plateau and then down to reach a wide col at 830m. Continue N, ascending gradually for a further 1½km to reach the 902m knoll. At this point turn NE, cross another knoll and continue in the same direction across the undulating plateau, gradually descending 30m before the final ascent of 50m to the flat summit of Carn na Caim.

To return to the starting point without having to walk along the A9 road, the only feasible option is to reverse the outward route. If a second car is available, a better finish to the tour is to return WSW from Carn na Caim for 1km to the top of the west facing slopes on the NE side of Coire Uilleim. Descend these slopes, which often have a good snow cover, and continue NW across the moorland to the A9 at the junction with the road to Dalwhinnie.

Skiing south-west from Geal-charn towards Loch Ericht and Ben Alder   *D.J. Bennet*

A'Mharconaich; 975m; (OS Sheet 42; 604764).
Geal-charn; 917m; (OS Sheet 42; 597783).
Beinn Udlamain; 1010m; (OS Sheet 42; 579740).
Sgairneach Mhor; 991m; (OS Sheet 42; 599732).
Starting point on the A9 road ½km south of the Drumochter Pass summit, (632756); altitude 450m.
Distance 20km. Height climbed 1200 to 1250m. Time 7-9 hours. Rating: ★★★/III.

This group of hills is well seen from the A9 road as one travels south of Dalwhinnie to Drumochter Pass. The rounded mass of Geal-charn, the most northerly of the group, has some large cairns just below the summit, and it is connected to A'Mharconaich which is seen from the north as a graceful rounded hill whose high eastern corrie is often edged in spring by a rim of snow. The northern slopes of Sgairneach Mhor form Coire Creagach, a steep and corniced bowl above Coire Dhomhain, at whose head Beinn Udlamain shows a long level skyline when seen from the road just south of Drumochter Pass.

The hills tend to be stony on their summits, and because of their windswept aspect the exposed ridges and slopes are often denuded of snow. Nevertheless, the traverse of them is a fine outing which is possible in most winters, the best conditions usually being found between March and mid-April. The starting point near Drumochter Pass is 450m above sea level, so little carrying of skis should be needed.

For the best downhill running the traverse should be done anti-clockwise round Coire Dhomhain. Cross the railway near a line of derelict cottages and reach the track up the corrie. Follow this for 2km then strike uphill N by good snow slopes until a fence is reached. Continue along this fence NW to the summit plateau of A'Mharconaich. The true summit is ½km NE along the level and often very stony plateau.

Geal-charn is the outlier of the group and stands 2½km NNW of A'Mharconaich to which it is connected by a bealach at 740m. To reach this bealach ski down the NW flank of A'Mharconaich on the line of the most westerly tributary stream of the Allt Coire Fhar which usually holds snow well. North of the bealach the ridge to Geal-charn becomes stonier as the summit is approached, and the best snow may well be found on the E side of the broad crest.

Beinn Udlamain is the next summit, and it is best approached by retracing one's tracks to the plateau of A'Mharconaich and then skiing SW along the line of the fence to the col at 860m. There are spectacular views from this part of the traverse to the hills of the Ben Alder and Ardverikie forests across the deep trench of Loch Ericht. If the ridge to Beinn Udlamain is windswept, the best snow may well be found on the SE flank above Coire Dhomhain, but the fence must be regained to reach the summit.

Continue S then SE down improving slopes which give a good run to the col at 810m between Beinn Udlamain and Sgairneach Mhor. There is rarely a problem of snow cover here and a direct line for the summit of the latter peak can be taken from the col.

The descent from Sgairneach Mhor to the Allt Coire Dhomhain is the highlight of the tour. First down the NE ridge — care being needed to avoid the cornices of Coire Creagach in bad visibility — to the first dip in the ridge at 740m, then due N keeping to the W of the burn down to the Allt Coire Dhomhain. Given good snow cover, there is a descent of almost 500m in 3km. Cross the stream and return along the track on its N side. If the stream is full and

Looking north-west from Sgairneach Mhor to Beinn Udlamain   *D.J. Bennet*

not snow-bridged low down, it would be prudent to aim for a higher crossing point when skiing off Sgairneach Mhor.

If the party has two cars, an alternative way to traverse this group is to start at Balsporran Cottages, 4 kilometres N of the Drumochter Pass summit. Cross the railway and follow the path W for ⅓km to cross the Allt Beul an Sporain; then climb directly up the NE ridge of Geal-charn, passing close to the prominent cairns near the summit. From there continue S to A'Mharconaich and complete the traverse as described above.

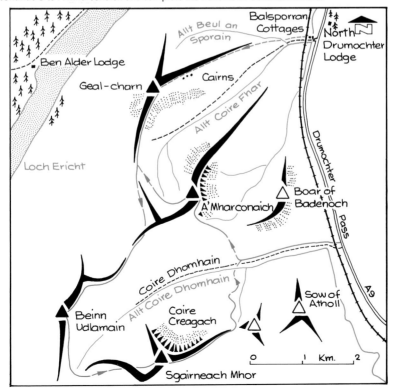

Meall Chuaich; 951m; (OS Sheet 42; 716879).
Starting point on the A9 at Cuaich (655866); altitude 350m. Distance 14km. Height climbed 600m.
Time 4-5 hours. Rating: ★★/II.

Meall Chuaich is rather a solitary hill on the east side of the A9 road, 9 kilometres north-east of Dalwhinnie. It is sufficiently far from its nearest neighbour, Carn na Caim, that only the very fit are likely to ski over both these hills in a single day for the intervening terrain is 10 kilometres of undulating featureless plateau. Meall Chuaich is most suitable, therefore, for a short half day's ski touring.

The usual route starts from the A9 road at Cuaich cottages and goes for 3½km along a private road which leads beside an aqueduct to a little power station, and beyond it to Loch Chuaich. A thin covering of snow is enough to make this part of the route skiable. Before reaching Loch Chuaich turn SE past a little bothy, following the track over a broken bridge across the Allt Coire Chuaich.

From there the route is up the WSW ridge of Meall Chuaich, a broad smooth ridge which gives easy skiing if it is snow covered. Unfortunately, it is the side of the hill which is most likely to lose its snow cover under the effect of mild SW winds, and it must be admitted that Meall Chuaich does not have the reputation of being a good snow holding hill. The ridge bears round E, steepens briefly and reaches the wide flat dome of the summit.

The descent is best made by the route of ascent, unless the snow cover is poor, in which case a steeper run further E down a very shallow corrie may give better skiing.

Another route to Meall Chuaich that makes a very long traverse if combined with the one described above is from Glen Tromie. There is, however, a 9km walk up the private road in this glen to Bhran Cottage, from where one climbs the long featureless ridge over Carn Thomas. This is a route for the long distance skier, best done with Nordic skis when there is deep snow cover in the glens.

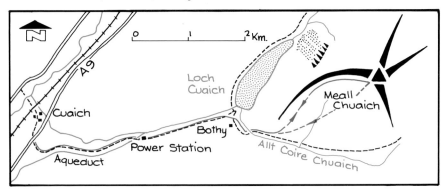

An Sgarsoch; 1006m; (OS Sheet 43; 933836).
Carn an Fhidhleir; 994m; (OS Sheet 43; 905842).
Starting point at the Linn of Dee (061897); altitude 370m. Distance 40km. Height climbed 920m. Time 12-14 hours. Rating: ★★★/II.

The traverse of these two distant, unfrequented hills is one of the longest tours described in this book, regardless of whether one approaches by the Dee, the Feshie or from Glen Tilt. The Linn of Dee is chosen as probably the best starting point, and the long easy gradient on the approach from there alongside the River Dee and the Geldie burn to the foot of the hills suggests that Nordic skis may be best suited for this tour.

Carn an Fhidhleir stands where the counties of Aberdeen, Inverness and Perth meet, in one of the most remote parts of Scotland. Both hills have mostly smooth gentle slopes, but the NE corries of An Sgarsoch are steep, and their rims often carry snow cornices. The approach up the Dee and the Geldie takes the skier up broad bare glens leading to distant hilltops where there is a great feeling of space.

From the Linn of Dee take the road W up Glen Dee, then SW from White Bridge, and finally W up the N side of the Geldie Burn. This leads in 12½km to a point opposite the ruined Geldie Lodge on the S side of the burn. A bulldozed track climbs WSW from the lodge towards Carn an Fhidhleir, and this track should be followed to its highest point. From there cross the Allt a' Chaorainn and climb SW straight to the top of Carn an Fhidhleir, 19km from Linn of Dee.

An Sgarsoch from Carn an Fhidhleir   M. Rawson

If the Geldie Burn at the lodge is high and not safe to cross, one can continue along the N side and usually find a safe crossing place in 2 or 3km where the burn is much smaller. From there it is easy to head directly to Carn an Fhidhleir, whose summit offers grand views of the wild bare country of the upper reaches of the Feshie, Tarf and Geldie, and of the great bulky Cairngorms to the north.

From the summit, even with patchy snow cover, a good run can usually be found by skiing just on the E side of the broad SSE ridge and then making a descending traverse to the 710m col below An Sgarsoch. A 300m climb follows to the broad top of that hill.

The best descent route is E along the wide ridge for about 1km until good slopes are found on the N side leading down to the Allt Coire an t-Seilich and Geldie Lodge. Lastly, there are 13km of glen to ski (or walk) back to Linn of Dee.

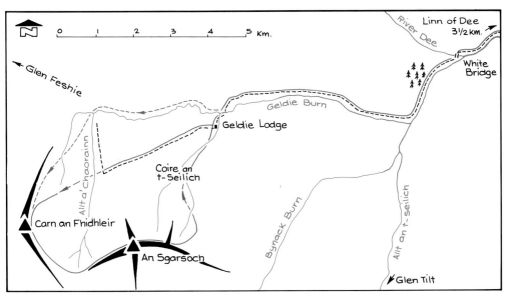

Beinn Dearg; 1008m; (OS Sheet 43; 853778).
Starting point at Old Blair (867666), 1½km north-west of Blair Atholl; altitude 150m. Distance 25km. Height climbed 1030m. Time 6-8 hours. Rating: ★★★/II.

This remote and isolated mountain lies 13km north of Blair Atholl, and is the south-western outpost of the great tract of high undulating plateau which stretches north and east towards Glen Feshie and the Cairngorms. Its ascent on skis is best suited to mid-winter days when snow lies low in the glens, making the long approach easy and more spectacular. This is a good tour for Nordic skis.

From Old Blair follow the private road NE past Blairuachdar Farm and Wood and take a left fork just before it emerges from the trees, where there is a fine view up Glen Tilt. A track then climbs into the glen of the Allt Slanaidh through another forest and leads to a small wooden bothy.

Beinn a' Chait lies 3km N and is easier to ascend to about the 850m contour than to traverse the W flank, as the height gained can be used to schuss to the col below the summit cone of Beinn Dearg. This rises 200m above a vast undulating plateau intersected by meandering snow-choked burns. The familiar skyline of the Cairngorms seems very distant across this high empty landscape.

From the summit it is worth skiing SW for 1½km for the view down Glen Bruar, but unless you decide to return via the bothy in the Allt Sheicheachan to Old Blair (longer and less scenic) do not lose too much height before turning SE towards Beinn a' Chait. The Allt Sheicheachan cuts deeply into the W flank of this hill, and holds a variety of attractive steep gullies. The slopes are, however, both convex and prone to windslab formation, so unless you are very sure of the snow conditions give them a wide berth by traversing high up above 800m.

From the SW shoulder of Beinn a' Chait there is a fine run of 300m down into the Allt Slanaidh, and the return through the woods with views across Glen Tilt to Beinn a' Ghlo is a delightful end to the day.

Alternative start: It may be possible to get permission from the estate office at Blair Castle to drive up Glen Tilt to Gilberts Bridge. From there cross the river and climb S up a track to join the route described above. This reduces the total distance by 4km.

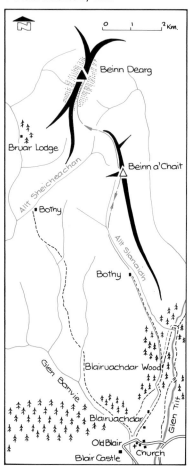

Approaching the Allt Slanaidh bothy en route to Beinn Dearg   R.Simpson

The approach to Ben Vrackie by the east ridge   R. Simpson

Ben Vrackie; 841m; (OS Sheets 43 and 53; 951633).
Starting point at a car park (944597) on the north side of Moulin village; altitude 150m. Distance 10km. Height climbed 690m. Time 3-4 hours. Rating: ★★★/II.

This small but interesting mountain makes a good short tour in deep midwinter when daylight is short and the snow may well reach down to the lower glen. The ascent along the line of the 'tourist path' is as good an approach as any. To reach this, leave Pitlochry by the A924 road to Kirkmichael, and immediately after the Moulin Hotel in the village of Moulin follow a steep narrow road on the left to a car park.

The path leads N from the car park through 1km of mixed birch and conifers to a stile. Beyond this an ascending traverse NE leads in 1½km to the col (520m) between Meall na h-Aodainn Moire and Creag Bhreac. From there traverse past Loch a' Choire and ascend to the summit of Ben Vrackie by its SE shoulder. The descent may be made following much the same line. It is particularly pleasant to end the run in the gloaming among the snow-burdened trees above Moulin.

Interesting alternative routes can be made if two cars are available. For example, if a car can be left, (or the party dropped off by an obliging driver), at the summit of the A924 road from Pitlochry to Kirkmichael, the ascent can be made starting at 380m. Climb NW over Carn Dubh and Carn Geal and then bear W along the final interesting E ridge of Ben Vrackie itself, which is narrow in places and requires care.

The descent from the attractively pyramidal summit can be made by the route described above, or alternatively NW from the summit towards Meall an Daimh. Do not ascend this outlier, but turn W and descend to the evocatively named farm of Druid from which a road goes down past Old Faskally House and under the new A9 road to the National Trust for Scotland's Visitor Centre at Killiecrankie. This is a convenient place where your second car, or the driver of your only car, can await you.

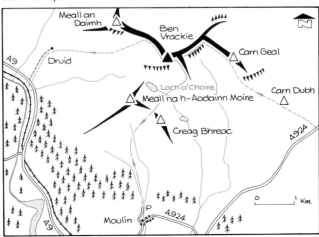

Looking south-west from Carn nan Gabhar to Braigh Coire Chruinn-bhalgain   J. Eames

Carn Liath; 975m; (OS Sheet 43; 936698).
Braigh Coire Chruinn-bhalgain; 1070m; (OS Sheet 43; 946724).
Carn nan Gabhar; 1129m; (OS Sheet 43; 971733).
Starting point at Loch Moraig at the end of the public road on the south side of Glen Fender (907672); altitude 340m. Distance (maximum round trip) 24km. Height climbed (traverse of peaks in both directions) 1640m. Time 7-10 hours. Rating: ★★★★/III.

Beinn a' Ghlo is a beautiful and mysterious mountain of many peaks, ridges and corries, which extends for 10km on the south-east side of Glen Tilt from Blair Atholl to the wild recesses of the Grampian mountains far to the north-east. When snow covered it gives one of the finest ski-mountaineering expeditions in Scotland, and it is very much an expedition for when you reach the outward end of the traverse at the highest summit, Carn nan Gabhar, you are a long way from civilization, and the sense of isolation is strong. The return may be a daunting prospect, particularly if the weather is bad or darkness is approaching.

The mountain is best approached from Blair Atholl, and a car can be taken as far as Loch Moraig at the end of the public road in Glen Fender, 1km before Monzie farm. At this point you are high on the moors SW of Carn Liath. Proceed directly towards the base of this peak and climb its ever steepening slopes by the best possible route. Snow cover is often thin, for this hillside faces SW and is very windswept. With a good snow cover, however, it is possible to zig-zag up without difficulty, although harscheisen will be useful if the snow is hard.

From the summit of Carn Liath there is a splendid run N then NE down the crest of the ridge for 1½km, traversing below Beinn Maol on its W side, and dropping 200m to reach the col below Braigh Coire Chruinn-bhalgain. From there ascend the steep SW shoulder to the summit of the Braigh 300m above.

Continue NE along the twisting main ridge, dropping about 70m, for 1km, then ski E down a good slope, steep at the top, for 150m to the col below Airgiod Bheinn at 847m, the Bealach an Fhiodha. From there make an ascending traverse to the N of Airgiod Bheinn to gain the main NE running ridge leading to Carn nan Gabhar, the main summit of the range, a climb of some 280m in 2km.

At this point you are some 12km from your car, and there is no easy return. To the north, south and east lie roadless desolations. In good conditions the best route is to follow the ridge back again to Carn Liath and enjoy the thrilling descent from there towards Loch Moraig and the glories of a winter sunset. This is well worth the 420m of reascent necessary to reverse the traverse. Another good ending would be to ski from Braigh Coire Chruinn-bhalgain down to Marble Lodge in Glen Tilt, where with prior permission from the Atholl estate office (and the payment of a modest fee) you may have a second car waiting.

If, however, the weather conditions are normal, with minimal visibility and a bitter wind blowing, it may be more expedient to return by a lower level route. Return to the Bealach an Fhiodha, and from there ski SSW down the glen leading to the Allt Coire Lagain. Before reaching this stream, at an altitude of about 450m, make a long contouring traverse SW below Carn Liath to reach the track between Loch Moraig and Shinagag. This can be a long and weary trudge in poor snow and gathering darkness, and once the track is reached there are still 2 or 3 kilometres to go to reach the road end.

Carn a' Chlamain; 963m; (OS Sheet 43; 916758).
Starting point in Glen Tilt at the bridge over the Allt Craoinidh (908720); altitude 280m. Distance 9km. Height climbed 690m. Time 3-4 hours. Rating: ★★/II.

Carn a' Chlamain is the highest hill on the north-west side of Glen Tilt, rising directly above Forest Lodge, and recognisable from afar by its pointed summit which appears just above the general level of the hills on that side of Glen Tilt. It is a short and easy ski ascent, provided one first gets permission from the estate office at Blair Castle (in return for the appropriate fee) to drive up Glen Tilt 1km past Marble Lodge to the bridge over the Allt Craoinidh.

From this point there are two easy routes up Carn a' Chlamain, one up the corrie of the Allt Craoinidh, and the other along the broad and smooth S ridge which merges with the SE ridge near the summit. A circular traverse combining these two routes is probably the best way to do the hill on skis. The 'summer route' by the path from Forest Lodge is not a ski route.

A track on the E side of the Allt Craoinidh leads for more than 1km up the corrie, and beyond it the going is very easy up smooth slopes leading W of the summit to avoid an area of steep scree. The broad NW ridge is reached about ½km from the summit, and one skis easily along this ridge, passing a rise with a cairn on it that might be mistaken for the top in bad visibility.

Ski SE from the summit (avoiding steep ground to the S) and in about 300 metres reach a broad level shoulder. Continue SE for ½km, then turn S and SW to ski easily along the broad ridge directly back to the bridge over the Allt Craoinidh.

It is quite possible to combine Beinn Dearg (see p68) and Carn a' Chlamain in a long day's traverse over the rounded hills NW of Glen Tilt. The distance between the two hills is about 7km, and midway there is a drop to 640m in Gleann Mhairc.

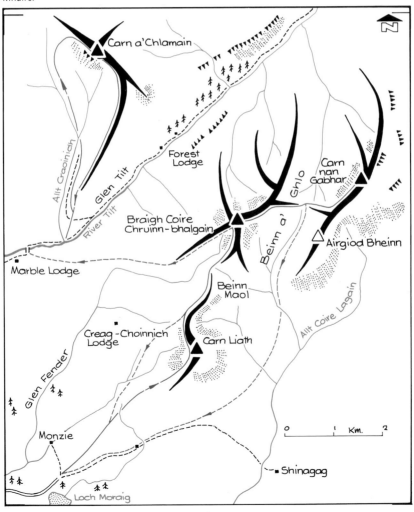

Carn an Righ from the east   *A. Watson*

Glas Tulaichean; 1051m; (OS Sheet 43; 051760).
Beinn Iutharn Mhor; 1045m; (OS Sheet 43; 045792).
Carn an Righ; 1029m; (OS Sheet 43; 028773).
Starting point for Glas Tulaichean at Dalmunzie Hotel (090713); altitude 360m. Distance 15km. Height climbed 750m. Time 4-5 hours. Rating: ★★★/III.
Starting point for Beinn Iutharn Mhor and Carn an Righ 1km north of the Cairnwell Pass on the A93 road (139781); altitude 650m. Distance 30km. Height climbed 1300m. Time 10-12 hours. Rating: ★★★/III.

These three mountains lie in the remote hinterland between the upper reaches of glens Tilt, Shee and Ey, a long way from the nearest public road, the A93 from Blairgowrie to Braemar over the Cairnwell Pass.

Glas Tulaichean is a massive sprawling mountain, from whose summit several broad smooth ridges drop south towards Glen Lochsie, an offshoot of Glen Shee. Carn an Righ and Beinn Iutharn Mhor are much more remote, the former being one of the least accessible mountains in the eastern Grampians.

Access to these mountains is either from the south, starting at Dalmunzie Hotel, 2½km NW of Spittal of Glenshee, or from the A93 road just north of the Cairnwell Pass. The traverse over one or more of them from the Cairnwell Pass to Dalmunzie is a very fine long expedition, calling for fitness, good snow conditions and the long days of spring.

The easiest ascent of Glas Tulaichean is from Dalmunzie. Beyond Glenlochsie farm the route lies up the long SE ridge which leads over several minor bumps to the summit which is poised above the splendidly corniced Glas Choire Mhor. A good ski-run southwards goes down the broad smooth ridge leading to Breac-reidh and the ruins of Glenlochsie Lodge. Alternatively, the corrie of the Allt Clais Mhor may offer a better snow cover. From the unwelcoming ruins of the lodge follow the track of the old narrow gauge railway back to Dalmunzie; the gradient is just enough to give a long easy schuss if the snow cover is adequate.

Glas Tulaichean may also be traversed from the Cairnwell via Loch nan Eun (see below) and its NE ridge. This is an excellent tour if a second car can be left at Dalmunzie.

Beinn Iutharn Mhor and Carn an Righ are best reached from the ski centre at the Cairnwell Pass at the head of Glen Shee. The length of this tour might justify taking the chairlift up The Cairnwell, although to climb to the col N of this hill takes less than half an hour. From the top of the chairlift ski down the NW ridge of The Cairnwell for 1km, then bear away W and SW along the ridge past Carn nan Sac to Carn a' Gheoidh, a high level route without much ascent or descent. Ski down the W ridge of Carn a' Gheoidh to the col before Carn Bhinnein, and from there descend W down to the Allt Elrig. There is now a 2km trudge to the summit of Carn a' Chlarsaich (871m) which is traversed to Loch nan Eun, a lonely high lochan in the heart of these mountains.

From the lochan ascend the NE ridge of Mam nan Carn to 900m and traverse W at this altitude to the col below Beinn Iutharn Mhor. A further 1km and 100m of climbing leads to the summit of this mountain. Return to the col and make a descending traverse SW to the col between Mam nan Carn and Carn an Righ. From there make your way up the E flank to the summit of Carn an Righ. This is a very remote mountain top, a long way from your starting point, and only the equally isolated Fealar Lodge, 3km away to the NW, is a possible refuge in bad weather.

A crossing of frozen Loch nan Eun   *D. Gaffney*

Ski down the ascent route to the Mam nan Carn col and traverse E across the S face of this hill to reach Loch nan Eun. From there three posssible routes exist. A low level route with the minimum of climbing on the way back to the Cairnwell Pass is round the N side of Carn a' Chlarsaich to the head of the Baddoch Burn, down this for 2km and then up to Loch Vrotachan and over the col between The Cairnwell and Carn Aosda to reach the ski slopes at Cairnwell. Another possibility, involving much more climbing, is to retrace the outward route over Carn a' Gheoidh. The third possibility, which might be the most prudent in really bad weather or approaching darkness, is to descend SE down the Allt Easgaidh to the bulldozed track in Gleann Taitneach followed by a weary trudge for two hours along the glen to Spittal of Glenshee.

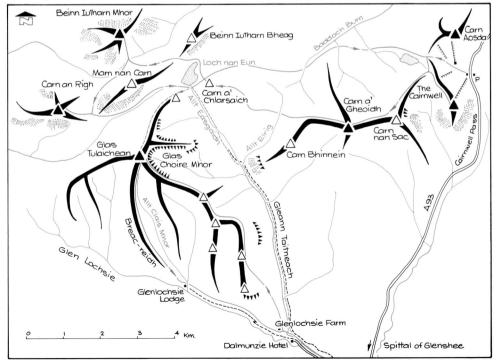

The descent from An Socach to the Baddoch Burn, looking towards Beinn a' Ghlo   D.J. Bennet

An Socach; 944m; (OS Sheet 43; 080800).
Starting point at the car park on the Cairnwell Pass on the A93 road (139781); altitude 650m. Distance 13km. Height climbed 800m. Time 5-6 hours. Rating: ★★/II.

An Socach is a long flat-topped hill between the head of Glen Ey and the Baddoch Burn, several kilometres west of the Cairnwell Pass. Its summit is a broad crescent-shaped ridge with the highest point at the W end, and a slightly lower cairn at the NE end. It gives an easy ski tour from the Cairnwell Pass, or alternatively from the foot of the Baddoch Burn, and the only difficulty may arise in bad visibility for the flank of An Socach above the Baddoch Burn is quite featureless, and it may be difficult when approaching up this slope to know whether or not it is corniced at the top.

From the Cairnwell Pass the first part of the route goes NW past the tows in Butchart's Corrie to the 800m col between The Cairnwell and Carn Aosda. To the W of this col a short descent leads to Loch Vrotachan, and the noise of the pistes is left behind. Pass the loch to the N or S depending on conditions, and ski down beside the burn flowing from it to the Baddoch Burn. The terrain is rough, and a good snow cover is needed for enjoyable skiing, possibly down the burn itself if it is snow-filled.

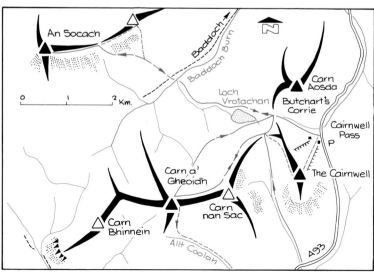

The Cairnwell from the head of Glen Clunie   *A. Watson*

Cross the Baddoch and climb the gradually rising slopes of An Socach which are easy-angled at first, then much steeper. If going to the highest point of the hill, bear WNW to reach the shallow open gully which leads up to the lowest point of the summit ridge. This gully, or the slope on its E side, gives an easy ascent without any cornice.

Once on the col an almost level ridge leads 1km W to the summit. If snow cover is thin and stones and boulders are in evidence, the best route may be on the S side of the ridge along which a continuous line of snow may form a cornice above the S face, so care is needed not to ski too close to the edge. The small summit cairn stands in the middle of the broad ridge.

If there is good snow cover it is pleasant to traverse the summit ridge for 2km to the NE top, and descend SE from there to the Baddoch Burn. Otherwise the ascent route described above should be used for the descent. Either way there is the possibility of a good downhill run of almost 400m to the Baddoch Burn. Finally, a climb of 250m is needed to regain the col E of Loch Vrotachan, and the last run of the day brings one back among the piste-bashers in Butchart's Corrie.

The Cairnwell; 933m; (OS Sheet 43; 135773).
Carn a'Gheoidh; 975m; (OS Sheet 43; 107767).
Starting point at the Cairnwell Chairlift on the A93 road (139781); altitude 640m. Distance 8½km. Height climbed 320m. Time 3-4 hours. Rating: ★★★/II or III.

This popular short tour usually starts from the top of the Cairnwell chairlift, thus reducing the total ascent to 130m. Purists may ascend through the pistes to the col just S of Butchart's Corrie.

For those wishing to avoid the congestion of the Glenshee ski area, particularly on a weekend, a long ascent (480m to The Cairnwell) may be made starting from the A93 S of The Cairnwell (134756) and ascending NNW up the glen between The Cairnwell and Carn nan Sac. The pay off is a longer run at the end of the day.

With good snow cover the most interesting route to Carn a'Gheoidh starts from the head of this glen at a small col SE of Loch Vrotachan and follows the ridge SW over Carn nan Sac (920m), which may be corniced in places, to where it abuts the summit slopes of Carn a'Gheoidh. On a fine day the views of the Cairngorms are magnificent and there are many sheltered hollows for sunbathing en route.

If the crest of the ridges are denuded of snow, it is usually possible, even late in the season, to work one's way round to the summit from Loch Vrotachan following burns and snow banks on the north facing slopes.

For most skiers Carn a'Gheoidh is the termination of the tour, from where a fast descent is made NE to skirt Loch Vrotachan and regain the col leading E into Butchart's Corrie. There are alternatives, however. The simplest descent is SE from the summit into the Allt Coolah, a long straightforward run after an initial (100m) steeper section. A finer alternative is to return to the summit of The Cairnwell as the sun is dipping in the west for the beautiful run either down the S ridge or the convex SW face.

Looking east from Mayar to Driesh   *W.D. Brooker*

Mayar; 928m; (OS Sheets 43 and 44; 241738).
Driesh; 947m; (OS Sheets 43 and 44; 271736).
Starting point at Auchavan at the end of the public road in Glen Isla (191696); altitude 360m. Distance 20km. Height climbed 870m. Time 7-8 hours. (2 hours less if Driesh is not included). Rating: ★★/II.

These two hills are the highest of a large expanse of rounded hills between glens Clova, Prosen and Isla. They lie close to Glen Clova, but the slopes on that side are steep, craggy and forested; not ideal for skiing. Glen Isla to the south-west gives a more distant starting point, and a long pleasant ski-tour over rolling hills, but beware of navigational errors in bad visibility which might lead you down to Glen Prosen, a long way from your car.

From Auchavan in Glen Isla cross the river and follow the track past Dalhally and up the SE side of the Glencally Burn for a further 2km. Continue up the burn on the S side of Sron Deirg and reach the plateau 1km W of Mayar. Do not head direct for the summit, as this involves a steep drop down to the Mayar Burn; instead, go N along the line

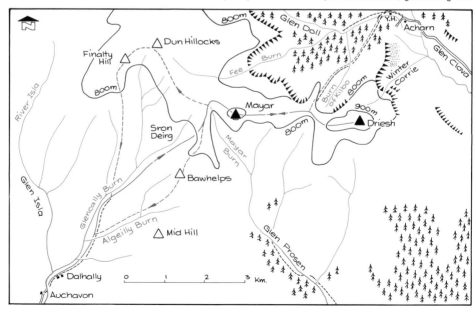

of a fence for a few hundred metres until an easy descent NE leads to the flat col 1km NW of Mayar. From there follow another line of fence posts to the summit.

To continue to Driesh, ski E for 2km to the Kilbo Pass at the head of Coire Kilbo. At this point a path reaches the pass from Glen Doll, but to ski up or down this path is not easy. To reach Driesh, 150m above the pass and 1½km distant, ascend SE for ½km to the plateau and then 1km E to the summit.

From Driesh one must return over Mayar from where the descent to Glen Isla is either by the uphill tracks or, if you want a slightly longer route and the conditions are favourable, along the ridge to Bawhelps and down by the Algeilly Burn. Another much longer variation is to ski NW from Mayar across the plateau to Dun Hillocks and down the S ridge of Finalty Hill to the Glencally Burn.

Carn an Tuirc, Cairn of Claise and Glas Maol from An Socach   *D.J. Bennet*

Glas Maol; 1068m; (OS Sheet 43; 166765).
Cairn of Claise; 1064m; (OS Sheet 43; 185789).
Carn an Tuirc; 1019m; (OS Sheet 43; 174804).
Starting point at the car park ½km north of the Cairnwell Pass (140778); altitude 660m. Distance 12km. Height climbed 600m. Time 4-5 hours. Rating: ★★★/III.

These three mountains, which are very accessible from the Glen Shee ski slopes, lie on the western perimeter of an extensive ski touring area which maintains an altitude of 900m for almost 16km north-east to the White Mounth and Lochnagar, and 10km east over the summits of the Angus hills. The circuit of Glas Maol, Cairn of Claise and Carn an Tuirc provides a good introduction to this area, and it is a short day even if one does not use the ski tows.

From the car park N of Cairnwell Pass follow a track E up the hillside on the S of the tows on Meall Odhar, and reach the summit of this hill. From there cross a wide col SE and ascend the NW shoulder of Glas Maol, which is steep at first, but leads to the easier slopes of the summit dome.

Alternatively, one can take the tows in two stages to Meall Odhar, ski down into Coire Fionn and take another tow up to the head of this corrie at 1000m, ½km N of the summit of Glas Maol.

Glas Maol is a fine viewpoint with an open southerly aspect. The south facing corrie which it shares with Little Glas Maol affords two fine ski runs, and the traverse of the Creag Leacach ridge, which is quite narrow in places, gives access to steeper skiing in the corrie on the SW side of that hill.

Under most conditions it is easy to follow the line of the fence and dyke N then NE from Glas Maol to Cairn of Claise, although high winds may blow the snow off the most exposed parts of the ridge and give frustrating skiing.

Continuing the circuit, there is an easy run N from Cairn of Claise followed by a short ascent NW to Carn an Tuirc and one of the classic ski runs in the Glen Shee area. From the summit ski N then NW down convex slopes leading into a shallow gully in which there are the remains of an old rope tow. Continue down the gully which leads W to join the Allt a' Gharbh-choire, which is followed on its N bank to the confluence with the Cairnwell Burn where there is a bridge leading to the A93 road.

Map on page 78.

Glas Maol; 1068m; (OS Sheet 43; 166765).
Cairn of Claise; 1064m; (OS Sheet 43; 185789).
Tolmount; 958m; (OS Sheets 43 and 44; 210800).
Fafernie; 998m; (OS Sheet 44; 215823).
Carn a' Coire Boidheach;1118m; (OS Sheet 44; 226845).
Lochnagar; 1155m; (OS Sheet 44; 244862).
Starting point at the car park ½km north of the Cairnwell Pass (140778); altitude 660m. Distance (finishing at Invercauld Bridge) 28km. Height climbed 1050m. Time 7-9 hours. Rating: ★★★★/II.

The vast undulating Mounth plateau that stretches north-eastwards from the Cairnwell Pass at the head of Glen Shee towards Lochnagar gives ski tourers, and particularly Nordic enthusiasts, one of the finest areas in the Scottish Highlands for long, high-level traverses. The terrain is distinctly Scandinavian in its feeling of space and remoteness, and in bad weather it has all the character of the Arctic wilderness, swept by storms, and in such conditions a traverse across this plateau will be a testing exercise in navigation. There may be few technical difficulties in the skiing (provided one does not stray into any of the steep corries or glens which surround the plateau), but the traverse from Glas Maol to Lochnagar is a major undertaking in terms of the distance to be covered over high ground, and an early start in the longer days of March or April is recommended.

Start from the S end of the Cairnwell car park and ascend E to reach the foot of the Meall Odhar ski tow, which is followed on its S side. From the top of the tow, which reaches close to the summit of Meall Odhar, descend slightly SE across a wide col and climb in the same direction towards Glas Maol. Snow conditions will dictate whether it is better to zig-zag up the steepest part of this slope on skins, or carry skis. Once up the short steep section continue SE for about ½km of easy ascent to the rounded summit. The cairn lies about 300 metres beyond a fenceline.

From the summit of Glas Maol ski N to meet the fenceline, which can then be conveniently followed all the way to Cairn of Claise. The ensuing descent towards Tolmount continues E along the line of old posts, and unless it is icy this 2km run across the plateau can be done in one long straight schuss. A small hollow is reached before ascending Tolmount by its SW flank.

Some rocks on the E side of Tolmount's summit are easily avoided before skiing down NE to cross Jock's Road (the footpath between Glen Doll and Glen Callater) just S of Knaps of Fafernie. The flat top of Fafernie, marked by a pimple-like cairn, is reached by climbing its easy-angled S ridge for 2km, and those who are keen enough may diverge ¾km ENE to include the slightly higher Cairn Bannoch in the traverse.

Ski easily N and then contour NE below Carn an t-Sagairt Mor and climb to the flat featureless top of Carn a' Coire Boidheach. Continue E, then NE across the White Mounth plateau which is defined on its N edge by the crags overlooking Loch nan Eun, and ascend more steeply to Lochnagar's secondary summit, Cac Carn Mor. The highest summit, Cac Carn Beag with its trig point set on a granite tor, is ½km NNW.

The return may be made by the same route back to the Cairnwell Pass, and on a good day with plenty of time this is quite feasible, though it does make a very long tour. A shorter and more logical ending is to ski from Lochnagar down through the Ballochbuie Forest to Invercauld Bridge in Deeside, provided you have a car waiting there. Return from Lochnagar along the outward route to the almost imperceptible col between The Stuic and Carn a' Coire

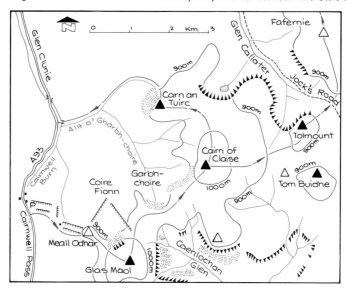

On the White Mounth, looking towards Lochnagar from The Stuic   G. Mackenzie

Boidheach and continue NW to reach the head of the Allt a' Choire Dhuibh. Ski down this stream to its junction with the Feindallacher Burn, and on the opposite bank reach the track which leads to Invercauld Bridge as described on the next page.

A more direct descent from Lochnagar to Ballochbuie can be made by skiing WNW from the summit down to Sandy Loch, but this is steep and should only be attempted with due care.

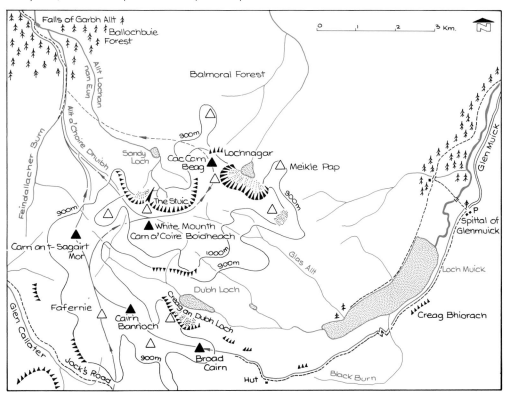

Cairn Bannoch (centre) and Carn an t-Sagairt Mor (right) from Broad Cairn   *A. Watson*

Broad Cairn; 998m; (OS Sheet 44; 240816).
Cairn Bannoch; 1012m; (OS Sheet 44; 223826).
Carn an t-Sagairt Mor; 1047m; (OS Sheets 43 and 44; 208843).
Starting point at the Spittal of Glenmuick (310852); altitude 410m. Distance 22km. Height climbed 810m. Time 7-9 hours. Rating: ★★★/III.

This tour makes a long traverse across the mountains on the south side of the White Mounth from Spittal of Glenmuick to Invercauld Bridge on Deeside, 3½km E of Braemar. It goes into the wild upper recesses of Glen Muick, above the great cliffs of Creag an Dubh-loch, over the rolling hills of the Mounth and finally down through the grand old pine forests of Deeside. Its length and the distance to be travelled over high plateaux make this a serious day's ski-touring, one that should be done in good conditions, for winter storms on the high Mounth are not to be encountered lightly.

From the car park at Spittal, the route goes along the track on the S side of Loch Muick, through scattered birches below Creag Bhiorach to a bridge over the Black Burn. Here one forks left up the hillside by a track which climbs in zig-zags to the plateau above. (The alternative route continuing by a path further along the loch-shore and then up to the plateau E of Corrie Chash is best avoided as the top part is steep, sometimes corniced and often icy).

Above the Black Burn the track goes along the plateau edge and then climbs to Allan's Hut (256808) SW of Corrie Chash. If the plateau edge and the ridge to the W lack snow, the ground to the S of the track usually holds more. Beyond Allan's Hut the route leads up to Broad Cairn, and the bulldozed track often holds snow when the stony slopes on either side are fairly snow-free. The top of the Broad Cairn is 1¾km WNW of Allan's Hut, and the actual summit is an exposed bouldery top which tends to be swept clear of snow, but there are usually big snowfields on either side.

From Broad Cairn an easy ski-run leads WNW to a 934m col, and gentle slopes beyond, usually well snow-covered, rise NW to Cairn Bannoch. The summit is a little rocky top, often peeping out as the only black spot among vast snowfields. The route now leads NW along a plateau to Carn an t-Sagairt Mor, where the view opens out to Glen Callater and Deeside. From there the best run is NNE across to and down the Allt a' Choire Dhuibh, and at the point where that burn joins the Feindallacher Burn one crosses to a track that gives a good run down into Ballochbuie Forest. Some of the steeper braes on the track offer short but exciting descents, and it is always a delight to ski down through the old pine forest, with magnificent views N to Beinn a' Bhuird and Ben Avon.

At the junction with another older road at (198895) turn right to pass close to the Falls of Garbh Allt on one's right, and another brae leads to a fork. The right track goes to the Balmoral stalker's house at Garbh Allt Shiel, and the left one goes through old pine forest and lastly past the beautiful hump-backed Old Bridge of Dee to the main road at Invercauld Bridge. From here there is a classic view looking back to the Old Bridge and the pine forest leading up to the snowy tops of Carn an t-Sagairt and the White Mounth.
Map on page 79.

Mount Keen and Braid Cairn (left) seen from the north-west   A. Watson

Mount Keen; 939m; (OS Sheet 44; 409869).
Southern approach: Starting point at Invermark at the end of the public road up Glen Esk at (444804); altitude 260m. Distance 18km. Height climbed 680m. Time 5-6 hours. Rating: ★★/II.
Northern approach: Starting point near Glen Tanar House at (474956); altitude 180m. Distance 27km. Height climbed 760m. Time 8-9 hours. Rating: ★★/II.

Appearing as a beautiful cone when seen from the north or south, Mount Keen stands out as a more distinctive hill than many higher tops in the Grampians. It is the most easterly of the 900m hills in Scotland, and offers very fine views over the low country of Aberdeenshire, Kincardineshire and Angus. The approach chosen may well depend on whether one is coming from the south by Glen Esk, or from the north along Deeside.

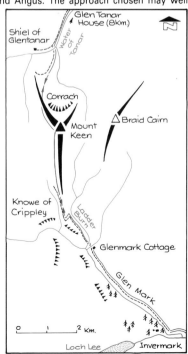

The shortest and easiest approach is the southern one, starting at Invermark in Glen Esk. Follow a private road up the NE side of Glen Mark and in 4km, with only 60m of ascent, reach Glenmark Cottage. This is a grand wild glen with many broken crags and steep slopes above its broad floor. Beyond the cottage, follow a bulldozed track up the Ladder Burn, and then by zig-zags onto the open slopes above. From there one can head straight for the top of Mount Keen by the broad, gradually steepening ridge.

The return by the same route usually offers a good run, and it is better not to stray to the E or W as some of the slopes are steep, rocky and often corniced.

A more interesting, but much longer route is from Glen Tanar near Aboyne. A good snow cover down the glen is necessary, otherwise one will have to carry skis for a long way. A private road goes from a car park near Glen Tanar House through beautiful natural pine forest up the glen and onto open moorland towards the Shiel of Glentanar, which has recently been opened as a bothy by the Glen Tanar Estate. From a point E of the Shiel a bulldozed track climbs S uphill to 530m, where one strikes off left to head S then SE round the corrie of Corrach to Mount Keen.

On the descent northwards be careful to avoid the steep rocky corrie of Corrach, where cornices often build up. The broad ridge to its W gives a good safe run down the ascent route to the glen and the shelter of its grand pine forest.

Climbing Morven from the north-east above the Howe of Cromar   A. Watson (sen)

Morven; 871m; (OS Sheet 37; 377040).

Dominating the Howe of Cromar and the lowland basin of Kinord, Morven stands at the eastmost extension of the Cairngorms. It offers an easier alternative to the higher mountains when snow-bound roads make them difficult of access.

The shortest and most attractive approach to the hill is on its E side, where the steep lower slopes hold snow particularly well. A minor road signposted to Groddie leaves the A97 1km S of Logie Coldstone at (433036) and leads E towards Morven. Start 2½km along this road at (411044), and from there ascent on skis over undulating pastureland, passing the deserted farmhouse of Balhennie either to the left or right. The open hillside is reached and the slope invites a rising traverse left for some 250m to an easement. Ascending westward round the upper basin of the Coinlach Burn, the E ridge of Morven may be gained. A line of fence posts leads to the summit, but the last 30m may be too rough for skis unless there is good snow cover.

Descend SE, swinging E across the snow-filled hollows of the Rashy and Coinlach Burn headstreams. The descent down the steep lower slope may be taken on the Coinlach side to Ballabeg, but further down the route is intersected by fences, so it is better to diverge NE to leave the hill at Balhennie and return to the starting point. (Distance 8km. Height climbed 650m. Time 3 hours).

An alternative and longer approach which is well suited to Nordic skis is from the south, leaving the A93 road 2km NE of Ballater. Start 150 metres E of Bridge of Tullich. Pass a large barn and go through a gate to join a track passing through the birch woods and young pine trees to enter the glen on the E side of Crannach Hill. Continue up this glen along a track and at its head cross a col to reach the wide upland basin of the Rashy Burn beyond which the steepening south-eastern slopes of Morven are climbed to the summit. (Distance 15km. Height climbed 680m. Time 4-5 hours).

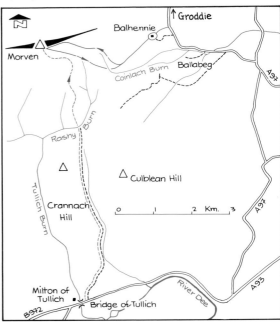

Culardoch; 900m; (OS Sheets 36 and 43; 193988).

Falling just short of Munro status, Culardoch is an outlier of Ben Avon, lying some 7km to its south-east and separated from it by the deep trench of Glen Gairn. It is a smooth sided, almost conical hill without crags or significant corries, and is not readily seen from Deeside.

Culardoch is best approached from the minor road which connects Inver with Invercauld Bridge via Felagie. If this road is blocked by snow it is necessay to start at Inver on the A93 road. If this is the case go by Tullochcoy and a track passing through birchwoods to slant upwards across the SW slopes of Leac Ghorm. This track is all that remains of the old public carriage road which used to cross from Deeside to Loch Builg; it was once the highest public road in the country, but now it expires among the mosses E of Culardoch.

If the Felagie road is open, follow it to Knockan or beyond until you can gain the farm track crossing the valley past Balmore. A right fork leads to a bridge over the Feardar Burn and the track climbs through birchwoods past Ratlich. The open hillside lies ahead and leads easily N to an undulating plateau of high ground where the route described in the preceding paragraph is joined, about 3km SE of Culardoch. The head of Glen Feardar forms a big corrie on the W, and the route skirts the rim of this corrie to reach the summit cone of Culardoch which rises on its far side. Although steep, it is only 150m before the easier angled final slope leads in a other 50m of climbing to the cairn.

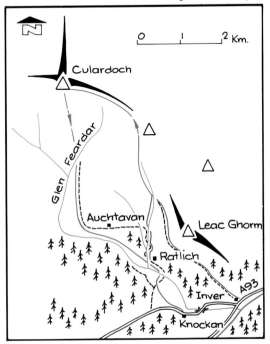

From there you can look along the cleft of Loch Builg to Glen Avon. To its left the entire N and W sector of the view is impressively filled by the vast white mass of Ben Avon, studded with rocky tors.

A recommended descent is to ski SSW into Glen Feardar, and exit eastward at about the 450m contour by the line of the track leading through the deserted farm of Auchtavan. The south facing slopes beyond are liable to thaw, and if refrozen will allow delightful skiing on bearing crust through open birchwoods to the valley floor below Ratlich. (Distance 14km. Height climbed 600m. Time 5-6 hours).

Ben Rinnes; 840m; (OS Sheet 28; 255355).

Ben Rinnes is the dominant hill in the lower Spey Valley, rising well above its lower neighbours and a prominent landmark from many distant viewpoints. It is high enough to hold snow well, particularly on the flanks of the east ridge, on one side or the other, depending upon the way the snow has drifted. Being a heathery hill, it needs a good snow cover to give good skiing, but in the right conditions it gives a pleasant short tour, for the B9009 road between Dufftown and Tomintoul passes close to the foot of the hill.

If the southern slopes have the better cover, ascend from Glen Rinnes, leaving the B9009 road near the post office at (273341). Reach the open hillside after crossing a sheep pasture and passing through some open scrub, and skirt the W end of Ben Rinnes Wood to gain the E ridge leading to the summit. This E ridge gives an excellent downhill run for Alpine or Nordic skis, but be sure to leave the ridge in time to clear the wood on your return to the glen.

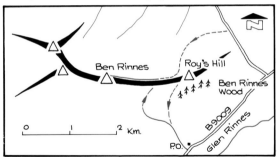

If the northern side of the E ridge has better snow cover, approach from the side road between Glen Rinnes and Aberlour on the E side of Ben Rinnes, provided this narrow road is not blocked by snow. Leave it at (282365) and follow a bulldozed track W for about 1km before turning S to join the E ridge W of Roy's Hill.

(Distance 6km. Height climbed 540m. Time 2-3 hours).

Clachnaben from the Glen Dye woods   *A. Watson*

In the depths of winter, during periods of general snow cover down to the valleys, the lower hills of north-east Scotland offer good varied hill country for ski touring, and snow conditions that cannot be matched in the high hills. They may also be more accessible than the higher Grampian and Cairngorm mountains when the roads to the latter are snow-bound. These low hills are smooth, lacking cliffs and generally gentle in slope, and as a result they are particularly suited to Nordic-style touring. In deep snow they become completely white, almost like arctic ice-caps, to a degree seldom seen on the high tops. In places there are scattered trees, birch and pine, regenerating naturally across the lower hillsides, and this gives a unusual character to the landscape, reminiscent of Lapland, which emphasises the Scandinavian character of touring on skis on these hills.

Clachnaben; 589m; (OS Sheet 45; 615865).
Mount Battock; 778m; (OS Sheets 44 and 45; 550845).

There is a fine tour from Glen Dye SW of Banchory to Mount Battock. Start just N of Greendams at (648902), about 1km off the B974 road, and ski W along a new road through the forest which leads onto recently afforested moor. A new forest road beyond continues to a stile over the electrified upper deer fence, and from there a

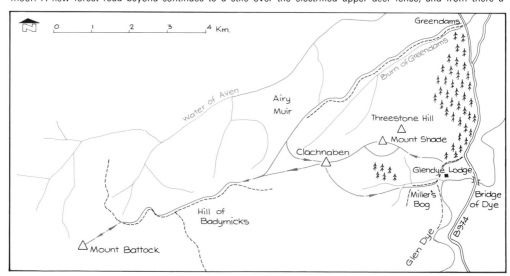

Clachnaben and Kerloch   R. Robb

bulldozed track zig-zags uphill to Airy Muir, from where there is an easy climb up to Clachnaben with its impressive big granite tor.

Mount Battock lies to the W along a broad, gently undulating ridge with the electrified deer fence on the S for most of the way. Stiles here and there offer access at track crossing points, and the wires also break occasionally due to icing. The top of Mount Battock, 7km from Clachnaben, dominates much of lower Deeside and gives fine views into Glen Esk. The return trip offers good runs back, first off Mount Battock, then down to Airy Muir and finally from there down to and along the forest road. (Distance 25km. Height climbed 740m. Time 6-7 hours).

When conditions are right, Clachnaben by itself gives an excellent half-day tour on Alpine or Nordic skis. Start just N of Bridge of Dye on the B974 road at (649867) and go W along a forest track. After leaving the wood follow a track NW through a recently afforested area onto the open moor below Threestone Hill. Next, contour round the S side of Mount Shade, or traverse it if snow conditions allow. A prominent glacial meltwater notch known as 'The Devil's Bite' marks the col from which the broad NE shoulder of Clachnaben leads to the summit. Complete the traverse by skiing SE and either step over the electric fence or cross it at a gate/stile where a track comes from the old wood to continue past Miller's Bog towards Glendye Lodge. (Distance 8km. Height climbed 400m. Time 3-4 hours).

Kerloch (534m), south of Banchory, is a fine viewpoint over the low country, and with a general snow cover it gives a good short tour. Start 2½km ESE of Strachan, just E of Moss-side at (699917). Much of the hill has been afforested, but a track from that point can be followed S up the lower moorland and through newly planted trees to (706889), and then up zig-zags to the open summit. The N face of Kerloch is steep enough to be a worthwhile descent on Alpine skis, provided that there is sufficient snow and frost to cover the marshy ground at the head of the Burn of Curran. (Distance 9km. Height climbed 420m. Time 2-3 hours).

Bennachie (528m) is one of the most familiar landmarks of the north-east, and it looks particularly fine when snow-covered. In hard winters when big snow falls have blanketed its rather stony lower slopes, it is one of the most accessible hills for ski touring in the north-east.

The route from the car park near Pittodrie NE of the hill is a good one, ascending briefly through the woods and then across open heather clad slopes to the top of the hill. Although the highest top of Bennachie is Oxen Craig, and Mither Tap is 10m lower, the latter receives far more visitors because of its spectacular summit tor and prehistoric fort. To reach it on skis requires a very deep snow cover. Another route starts at the car park near Tullos SE of Bennachie and takes a path W through the forest for 2km before turning N up boulder strewn ground onto the hill.

With or without Mither Tap, the best ski tour of Bennachie is the complete traverse from W to E over the main tops from the B992 road near Towmill to the car park near Pittodrie, a distance of some 10km and best suited to Nordic skis.

The South Top of Beinn a' Bhuird from the pinewoods of Glen Quoich   G. Mackenzie

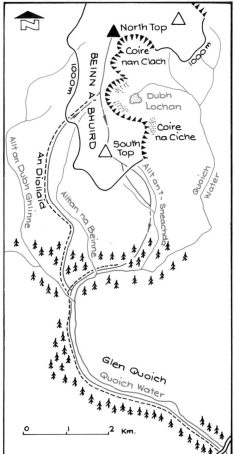

Beinn a' Bhuird; 1196m; (OS Sheets 36 and 43; 093006).
Starting point just west of the Quoich bridge (117911) 2km ENE of Mar Lodge; altitude 330m. Distance 26km. Height climbed 920m. Time 8-10 hours. Rating: ★★★/III.

Beinn a' Bhuird offers a magnificent tour through splendid glen and mountain scenery, with a spacious high plateau and wild plunging corries around it. The plateau is very exposed and shelterless, and the cliffs heavily corniced, so one needs to pick the day well and be sure of good navigation.

Starting a short distance W of the bridge over the Quoich Water, follow the bulldozed track on the SW side of this river through old pine and birch woods. In 5½km the track crosses the Allt an Dubh Ghlinne at a ford, but on skis one may have to look up or down stream for an easier way across. It is often possible to cross a shallow snow-covered burn on skis when one would break through on foot.

The track continues N up to and through a pine wood, and climbs in a few zig-zags onto the projecting ridge of An Diollaid. This track may well hold snow even if the surrounding slopes are bare, and it continues N across a saddle where, if there is insufficient snow for skiing, a diversion a short distance to the E may give better snow cover. (Watch not to go onto the big steep slope on the W side of the Alltan na Beinne near (077974) which may be corniced).

The route now goes NNE up the broad ridge ahead, and again its E side tends to hold more snow in the hollow of the Alltan na Beinne, but still beware of corniced slopes close to the burn. Eventually one comes onto the plateau near the col between the North and South tops where there is a spectacular view down the cliffs to the Dubh Lochan. Gentle slopes lead N across the plateau and so to the North

On the corniced edge of the Beinn a' Bhuird plateau   *R. Ferguson*

Top, the summit Beinn a' Bhuird, 13km from the Quoich bridge.

On the return journey there is a good run down the W side of the Alltan na Beinne, but the lower part of this stream E of An Diollaid sometimes has little snow. The best return route in good weather and snow is S along the plateau to the South Top, then down slopes on the W of the Allt an t-Sneachda where there is a continuously steep and exhilarating descent of 550m to the pine wood of Quoich. There the upper end of the track in Glen Quoich is reached, and this track can be followed W to the Allt an Dubh Ghlinne ford and back to the Quoich bridge by the outward route.

Ben Avon (Leabaidh an Daimh Bhuidhe); 1171m; (OS Sheets 36 and 43; 132019). Three routes are described, one starting point is in Glen Avon at Birchfield (167148); altitude 350m. Distance 35km (Possible to do 20km by bicycle). Height climbed 850m. Time 10-12 hours. Rating: ★★★/III.

Three different routes are commonly used to reach this remote and huge plateau mountain, all involving lengthy approaches up the surrounding glens. No matter which way is chosen, the ski ascent of Ben Avon is a very long expedition, best done in late March or April when the days are long enough.

If road conditions allow, the best way is that from the N, where a bicycle may be used for 10km from the locked gate at Birchfield along the private road up Glen Avon to a point about 1km beyond Inchrory. The NE spur of Ben Avon rises from there, but if it is bare of snow it may be better to continue along the road for 1½km and then head due S to the col W of Meall Gaineimh. Keep on the E side of the crest-line past East Meur Gorm Craig to reach the main plateau on Big Brae, and then bear SW to gain Mullach Lochan nan Gabhar. Alternatively, the same point may be reached by continuing 1km further up Glen Avon and climbing into Caol Ghleann from the head of which a long-lasting snowfield rises to the plateau. The large summit tor of Ben Avon lies to the SW across a shallow scoop in the plateau which may be crossed or skirted round its N side.

The return may be made by either of the two routes described above. That by Caol Ghleann gives a continuous downhill run from the plateau to the River Avon of 600m. The northern corries hold much snow, but they are steep-sided and in places contain crags of Cyclopean aspect. Be watchful for avalanche danger. The plateau itself is complex and demands accurate navigation in poor visibility. Be particularly careful not to ski down either of the streams which converge to fall over a cliff at (159026).

From the east, Ben Avon may be approached up Glen Gairn, and a bicycle is useful along the estate road past Corndavon Lodge to the ruined Lochbuilg Lodge. From there ascend steeply to Carn Dearg and follow the ridge SW over Carn Drochaid, then climb a long slope to gain the main plateau at the striking tor of Clach Choutsaich. Continue NW across fairly level ground to join the preceding route, and either traverse across or around the plateau basin to reach the summit on its far side.

On the return leave the uphill route before Carn Drochaid and ski down the N side of the Allt Phouple into Glen Gairn, a descent of over 600m from Clach Choutsaich.

Ben Avon from the summit of Morrone   *W.D. Brooker*

The third approach to Ben Avon is from the Dee Valley to the S, and it may be the only one practicable if minor roads are snowbound. Occasionally climbed with Beinn a' Bhuird in a lengthy excursion via Glen Quoich, it is more usual to start from Invercauld Bridge, 3½km E of Braemar. From Keiloch, where the public road ends, take the estate road NW past Alltdourie and up the Slugain to reach Glen Quoich. Continue N to The Sneck, the col at the head of this glen between Beinn a' Bhuird and Ben Avon. Climb E steeply from the col, and continue NE for 1½km across the undulating plateau to the summit. The return may be varied by skiing SW then S to Carn Eas, and enjoying a steep 400m descent to Glen Quoich.

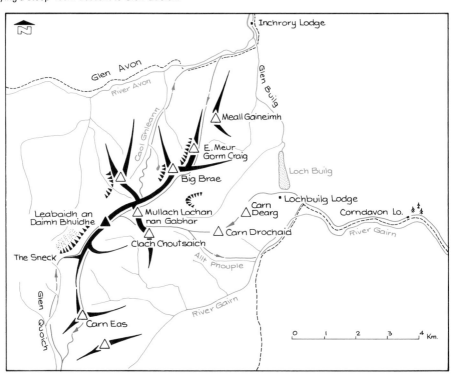

Looking north-east from Beinn Bhreac towards Derry Cairngorm, with Ben Macdui beyond   H.M. Brown

Beinn a' Chaorainn; 1082m; (OS Sheets 36 and 43; 045013).
Beinn Bhreac; 931m; (OS Sheets 36 and 43; 058971).
Starting point ¾km east of the Linn of Dee at the foot of Glen Lui (068898); altitude 370m. Distance 28km. Height climbed 800m. Time 8-10 hours. Rating: ★★★/II.

These two hills, situated between the great massifs of Ben Macdui to the west and Beinn a' Bhuird to the east, are relatively unfrequented, but they offer good ski touring and very fine views of the higher Cairngorms around them. They are bare hills, with mostly gentle slopes and a wide plateau between them, but in places they plunge steeply into the pine-studded glens on either side.

The recommended approach to these hills is the same as that for the Ben Macdui – Derry Cairngorm tour, namely up Glen Lui from the locked gate at its foot to Derry Lodge. Continue up the bulldozed track through the pine woods on the E side of the Derry Burn for just over 2km, and then leave the glen and climb N up Coire an Fhir Bhogha which steepens at its head before the plateau is reached at Craig Derry. Ski across this great flat plateau, called the Moine Bhealaidh, bearing NE, then N and finally NNW to hold to the highest ground, and so up steepening slopes to the summit of Beinn a' Chaorainn.

If there is good snow cover right down into Glen Derry, a pleasant alternative to the climb up Coire an Fhir Bhogha is to ski right up the glen, first through the pines on the W side of the burn and then on the E side along the bare upper reaches until the Glas Allt Mor is reached. Climb diagonally NE up the steep spur on the W side of the narrow corrie of the Glas Allt Mor. This steep nose leads onto the plateau at (040995), and the top 100m are too steep for skiing; crampons might be needed. Beware also of avalanche-prone slopes to the E. Once on the plateau bear NNE across level ground for 1km, then up steepening slopes to the summit.

The corrie SE of the summit of Beinn a' Chaorainn usually holds much snow, offering a good run down to the Moine Bhealaidh. At the S end of this plateau, 5km from Beinn a' Chaorainn, Beinn Bhreac rises gently to a pair of tops, the SE one being the higher.

From Beinn Bhreac the quickest descent to Glen Derry is SW directly down to the pine woods. However, it is probably better (unless a storm is blowing) to stay on high ground for a few kilometres more. To do this, ski SSW for 1km to the col W of the Poll Bhat, then S on a horizontal traverse across the W flank of Meall an Lundain. Continue skiing S, descending at an easy angle along the burn (not named on the OS 1:50000 map) which flows into Glen Lui. Near its foot this burn goes through a narrow little gorge which should be avoided on the last run down to the glen.

Map on page 91.

The Cairngorms from Morrone, with Ben Macdui and Derry Cairngorm in the centre   *W.D. Brooker*

Ben Macdui; 1309m; (OS Sheets 36 and 43; 989989).
Derry Cairngorm; 1155m; (OS Sheets 36 and 43; 017980).
Starting point ¾km east of Linn of Dee at the foot of Glen Lui (068898); altitude 370m. Distance 29km.
Height climbed 1150m. Time 9-11 hours. Rating: ★★★★/III.

Ben Macdui, highest of the Cairngorms and standing in the centre of the massif, is one of the best ski mountaineerng hills in Scotland, with a great wealth of glen, corrie, plateau and loch scenery. It is a good tour on its own, but when linked with Derry Cairngorm it gives a long hill day that is particularly full of variety and interest.

This tour starts with a long approach up Glen Lui from the locked gate at the foot of the glen, ¾km E of the Linn of Dee. Skiing along this glen on a fine day is delightful, as there are magnificent old pines in the lower part, and grand spacious views higher up. Derry Lodge stands in a plantation at the top of Glen Lui, 5km from the start.

After crossing the Derry Burn by a footbridge just beyond the lodge, the route goes W by the path up Glen Luibeg on the N side of the Luibeg Burn. This path leads through ancient scattered pines for 2½km to a point E of a small copse, where a branch path slants up right, and is followed N for 2km to a junction of streams. The route then goes NW up the broad ridge of Sron Riach between the two streams, giving fine views southwards to the Perthshire hills. At 1110m the ridge flattens out at the top of Sron Riach, and one comes to the cliffs of Coire an Lochain Uaine on the right. The edges of these cliffs are usually heavily corniced, and the nearby ground is bouldery, so it may be best to ski up about a hundred metres W of the edge on smoother ground that is usually well covered with snow. This soon leads to the plateau at the top of the Allt Clach nan Taillear, and the summit of Ben Macdui is ¾km WNW up easy slopes.

The best return route follows roughly the line of the path towards Loch Etchachan, E for 1km then NE. In mist or storm, navigation has to be very good from the summit across the plateau to the slope NE of Stob Coire Sputan Dearg, and special care is needed near the cliff edge to avoid going over the cornices. Once this slope is reached there is a fine, but not steep ski run towards Loch Etchachan. One should not, however, ski right down to the loch, but bear right (E) to reach the 1053m col W of Creagan a' Choire Etchachan.

If bad weather comes on, an easy way down from this col is S along the burn in Coire Sputan Dearg and so to Glen Luibeg. A longer bad weather alternative is to ski down to the E end of Loch Etchachan and down into Coire Etchachan towards upper Glen Derry.

The route to Derry Cairngorm, however, leads SE across the flank of Creagan a' Choire Etchachan to the 1014m col to its S, and then on to the bouldery summit of Derry Cairngorm. The slopes on the E side have fewer boulders and generally better snow cover, and this is particularly so on the descent from Derry Cairngorm. Ski down to the E of the top of Little Cairngorm (1040m) and then down the broad ridge to the 833m col N of Carn Crom. A short climb leads to the E shoulder of Carn Crom above Coire na Saobhaidh with its slabby cliffs falling towards Glen Derry, and the edge of this corrie, which is often corniced, should be avoided.

Finally, ski SE down the broad ridge towards Derry Lodge. Inspection on the outward journey will have shown the best run off the hill, either to the W or the NE of the rocky knob of Creag Bad an t-Seabhaig. The last run through the pines down to the footbridge at Derry Lodge may well be the most interesting of the day, and the long langlauf down Glen Lui, possibly with the wind to help one, makes a good finish to this tour.

An excellent variation of this tour is to make the traverse from Deeside to the Spey Valley over Derry Cairngorm, Ben Macdui and Cairn Gorm. This is probably the most popular crossing between the two great valleys of the Cairngorms, but it does require two cars or, better still, a friendly driver. If you chose to start from the Linn of Dee and want to include Derry Cairngorm, follow the route described above in reverse, going first to Derry Cairngorm and then to Ben Macdui. From there a long easy run N across the plateau leads down to Lochan Buidhe (hidden under the vast snowfields) and then NE to the rim of Coire an t-Sneachda. There, on a good day, you will meet the skiers who have come up from the Spey Valley, and their tracks will lead you to Cairn Gorm. Finally, ski N to the hemispherical dome of the Ptarmigan Restaurant, and end the day dodging the piste bashers among the moguls of the White Lady or Coire na Ciste – a very different scene from the vast silent landscape of Ben Macdui.

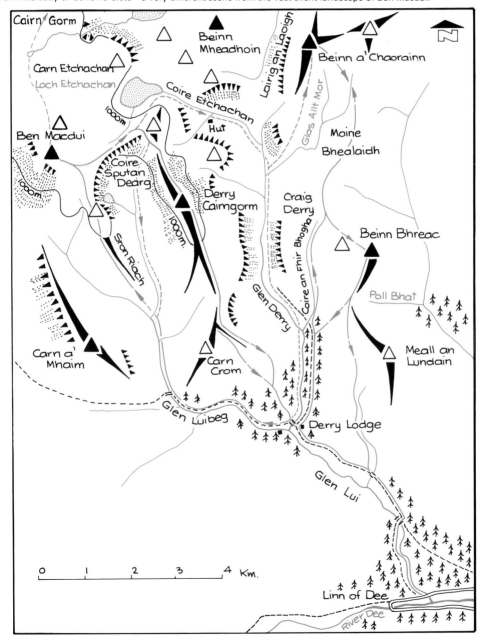

The descent from Ciste Mhearad to The Saddle en route to Bynack More   H.M. Brown

Bynack More; 1090m; (OS Sheet 36; 042063).
Starting point either at the car park in Coire na Ciste (999075); altitude 550m, or at the car park in Coire Cas (990060); altitude 630m. Distance 15km. Height climbed 550m (using chairlift). Time 5-7 hours. Rating: ★★★/IV.

This is an interesting tour through complex and varied mountain terrain which may require good route-finding and judgement of snow conditions. By using the chairlifts 1110m of downhill skiing can be enjoyed for only 550m of climbing.

From either car park ski or take the uplift to the Ptarmigan Restaurant at 1090m on Cairn Gorm. From there ski SE to the broad saddle above Ciste Mhearad. Cross this saddle and descend, avoiding snowholes, in the line of the burn for about 100m until the angle steepens, then make a descending traverse S across easier slopes into another shallow stream bed. This leads down until another traverse line well below an expanse of slabs leads to The Saddle overlooking Loch Avon. (If there is a danger of avalanches from the slabs, descend more directly to the Garbh Allt and ascend S to The Saddle). From there a broad, easy-angled ridge leads NE over A'Choinneach (1017m) to the Little Barns and Bynack More.

From the summit of Bynack More bear NW (skis may have to be carried over boulders initially) to the col between Bynack More and Bynack Beg, and then enjoy the 450m descent down the Allt a' Choire Dhuibh to Strath Nethy. If there is sufficient snow low down in Strath Nethy, one may ski down this glen past Bynack Stable and through Ryvoan Pass to Glenmore Lodge (8km). However, to return to the day's starting point climb W out of Strath Nethy on the S side of the gorge below Stac na h-Iolaire to reach the crest of the long N ridge of Cairn Gorm. Once the ridge is gained head SW above a rectangular plantation, making a descending traverse below Coire Laogh Beag and Coire Laogh Mor to the car park at the foot of Coire na Ciste.

The above tour is recommended in safe snow and reasonable visibility. Otherwise, the approach to Bynack More from Glenmore Lodge by Ryvoan Pass and Strath Nethy, though longer (20km; 750m of ascent) is pleasant and straightforward if snow lies down to the glen.

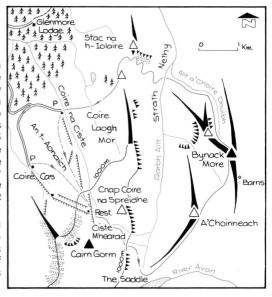

Skiing south-west from Cairn Gorm towards Stob Coire an t-Sneachda   D.J. Bennet

Cairn Gorm; 1245m; (OS Sheet 36; 005040).
Cairn Lochan; 1215m;(OS Sheet 36; 985025).
Starting point at the car park in Coire Cas (990060); altitude 630m. Alternatively at the Ptarmigan Restaurant (005049); altitude 1080m. Starting from the Ptarmigan Restaurant: Distance 9km. Height climbed 360m. Time 3-4 hours. Rating: ★★★/III.

Throughout the winter, and particularly at weekends, Coire Cas and Coire na Ciste, two of the northern corries of Cairn Gorm, are crowded with downhill-only skiers, queuing endlessly for uphill lifts and hurtling down the icy moguls of the White Lady and other popular pistes. Many a downhill skier, tiring of this way of life, must have looked above and beyond these crowded slopes to the lofty summit of Cairn Gorm and the high plateaux beyond, and longed for the peace and solitude of those high places. For them, their first ski tour might well be the climb to the summit of Cairn Gorm, the traverse south-westwards along the rim of Coire an t-Sneachda to Cairn Lochan on the edge of the great plunging cliffs of Coire an Lochain, and the return by the long easy ski run down Lurcher's Gully.

Although this is a short tour, and very suitable as an introduction to Scottish ski-mountaineering, it is not one to be undertaken too lightly. Adequate mountain equipment, map and compass are essential, for a sudden storm might blot out the landscape and in such conditions the exposed and featureless plateaux of the Cairngorms are not places for inexperienced or ill-equipped skiers. On the other hand, on a fine afternoon or evening in spring, there is no better contrast after a crowded day on the pistes than this excursion round the Northern Corries.

If starting from the Coire Cas car park, climb E for a short distance onto the rounded crest of the Sron an Aonaich ridge and continue up this ridge to the hemispherical dome of the Ptarmigan Restaurant at the top of the White Lady chairlift. Continue 1km S, keeping E of the direct line if the snow cover is thin, to the summit of Cairn Gorm where superb views of the whole range open out to the S and W. The slope dropping W to the flat col at the head of Coire Cas is swept by westerly winds and boulders are often exposed, calling for careful skiing.

Beyond the col the broad level ridge leads S then SW with a short climb to Stob Coire an t-Sneachda (1176m). If the snow on the crest of the ridge is thin, and skiing among the rocks difficult, take a lower line to the SE where the snow cover is usually better. Descend WSW to the col between the head of Coire Domhain and the innermost corner of Coire an t-Sneachda. On the right (N) ski tracks may lead to the edge of the steep slope above Coire an t-Sneachda, and some tracks may even continue down it. This descent comes into the category of 'extreme skiing', a 150m drop at an average angle of about 40°, suitable only for experts with the skill and confidence to ski such slopes.

Continue uphill for a short distance W to the level plateau of Cairn Lochan, whose summit is a few hundred metres further WSW, reached about one hour after leaving Cairn Gorm. Beware of cornices only a few metres NW of the cairn.

Ski on WSW for ⅓km, keeping well away from the edge of the cliffs on one's right, until beyond Coire an Lochain, then descend NW down a wide slope where there is plenty of room for wide turns and traverses. At the foot of this slope continue N across level ground for ¾km, then descend again, still N, to the head of the Allt Creag an Leth-choin. The shallow open corrie holding this stream is known among skiers as the Lurcher's Gully, and it is usually well filled with snow until late in spring, giving a long easy ski run.

If one wants to avoid any climbing on the way back to Coire Cas, it is necessary to leave the Gully at about 800m altitude and make a long descending traverse NE across the lower level expanse of Coire an t-Sneachda. Alternatively, if the snow cover is good, one may yield to the temptation to ski on down Lurcher's Gully for a further one or two kilometres, but this will entail a final climb back up to the car park in Coire Cas.

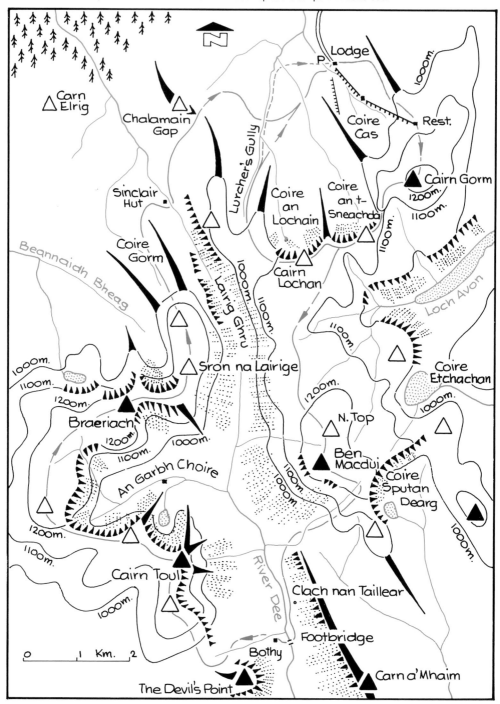

Looking towards Braeriach from the plateau between Cairn Lochan and Ben Macdui   *D. Snadden*

Cairn Gorm; 1245m; (OS Sheet 36; 005040).
Ben Macdui; 1309m; (OS Sheet 36; 989989).
Cairn Toul; 1293m; (OS Sheets 36 and 43; 964972).
Braeriach; 1296m; (OS Sheets 36 and 43; 953999).
Starting point at the Coire Cas car park (990060); altitude 630m. Distance 32km. Height climbed 2100m. Time 12-15 hours. Rating: ★★★★★/IV.

This is one of the finest ski-mountaineering tours in Scotland, a great expedition which gives magnificent views and skiing and a big variety of mountain scene. The skier will have a great feeling of space as he moves rhythmically across the high plateaux, and will get exciting descents as he plunges down the big corries. It is a serious tour and should be attempted only in good weather, and only by fit and experienced ski mountaineers who are used to navigating across featureless terrain in bad visibility. Ice axe and crampons may be needed.

The finest ways to do this tour are to start and finish at Whitewell near Inverdruie on Speyside, or at Derry Lodge in Deeside, but both these starting points involve quite long approaches, possibly on foot. Most people will probably prefer the easier access provided by the road up to Coire Cas on Cairn Gorm, and some may even take the chair-lift up to the Ptarmigan Restaurant only 170m below the top of Cairn Gorm.

The best time of year to do this tour is in spring, late March or April, when the daylight hours are long enough and there is the chance of spring snow on the mountains to give excellent skiing conditions. Provided the snow is down to about 600m, it should be possible to ski practically all the way.

Starting from the Coire Cas car park (or the Ptarmigan Restaurant) the first part of the tour follows the route up Cairn Gorm and across Stob Coire an t-Sneachda (described for the Northern Corries traverse on the previous pages) as far as the col at the head of Coire Domhain. If there is a lack of snow along the edge of the plateau above Coire an t-Sneachda, a lower traverse to the SE may give better conditions.

From the head of Coire Domhain the route goes SW, traversing horizontally across the SE slopes of Cairn Lochan to Lochan Buidhe, which under a deep cover of snow may well be indistinguishable from the rest of the flat, featureless plateau. Continue SSE gradually uphill towards the North Top of Ben Macdui; a steeper rise leads across its W side and finally a gentle ascent brings one to the huge cairn on Ben Macdui, 6½km from Cairn Gorm.

The descent from Ben Macdui down to the depths of the Lairig Ghru over 700m below is one of the finest and most challenging ski-runs in the Scottish mountains, and the route should be carefully chosen. Most of the SW slopes facing Cairn Toul are steep, bouldery and in places prone to avalanche. The best and safest way is to ski ESE for ½km to the flattish ground at the top of the Allt Clach nan Taillear (the burn of the tailors' stone), and carefully prospect the steeper part of the burn below. If the snow is not avalanche-prone, an exciting descent can be made all the way down the burn. Otherwise a safer route is down the broad ridge to the SE of the burn, crossing to the N side at about 800m, (the same height as the Carn a' Mhaim col ½km to the S). Lower down, where the burn turns W, cross back to its S side and make a descending traverse SSW towards the Clach nan Taillear and continue,

Skiing from Ben Macdui down to the Lairig Ghru by the Allt Clach nan Taillear   R. Ferguson

possibly on foot for this is the lowest point of the traverse, to the footbridge over the River Dee and Corrour Bothy on its other side.

From Corrour the route goes W by the path up Coire Odhar. A short steep part at the top, where the path zig-zags, often carries a small cornice, but this can be bypassed by going further S, nearer The Devil's Point. This top section is sometimes icy and crampons may be needed; alternatively, if the snow is soft it may be prone to avalanche. It is usually best to climb the last 100m on foot, with skis on your rucksack.

At the top of this steep climb a fine view suddenly opens out to the W across the extensive plateau of the Moine Mhor. Turn NW and climb to Stob Coire an t-Saighdeir (1213m), the south top of Cairn Toul, up a smooth slope which usually carries big snowfields. The top itself, and the ridge beyond it along the cliff top of Coire an t-Saighdeir, are bouldery and often largely clear of snow, in which case a better line will probably be found on the W side of the ridge. The last slope up to the top of Cairn Toul is also bouldery and usually only has a good snow cover after heavy snowfalls. It may be necessary to carry skis up to the cairn of this, the finest peak of the 'big four' Cairngorms.

Ski W off the peak, then WNW to the 1140m col below Sgor an Lochain Uaine, the Angels' Peak (1258m), from where there is a grand view down to Lochan Uaine and across An Garbh Choire to the bowl of Coire Bhrochain with Braeriach above it. If the upper slopes of Sgor an Lochain Uaine are not well covered with snow, it may be best to traverse horizontally W across the S side of this peak to reach the col to its W, the lowest point between Cairn Toul and Braeriach.

The route continues round the rim of the precipices of Garbh Choire Mor and Garbh Choire Dhaidh, whose cliffs carry massive cornices, so ski uphill along a safe line well back from the edge. Once up on the high plateau near the 1265m south-west Top of Braeriach you will feel the far-ranging space around you, a great contrast to the plunging amphitheatre of an Garbh Choire, the snowiest place in Scotland. Continue NNE down a very gentle slope for 1km to a flat expanse where the infant River Dee, probably hidden under a deep covering of snow, flows SE to tumble in the Falls of Dee down into An Garbh Choire. Then bear ENE up an equally gentle rise for 1km to the summit of Braeriach, where the cairn is only a few metres from the cornices above Coire Bhrochain near the deep indentation of West Gully. From this top there is a remarkable change of view, looking down to the forests and lochs of Strath Spey.

The descent goes ENE at first, down a wide slope, then E for a short distance along a narrowing ridge where the steep slopes of Coire Beanaidh on the left and the cornice of Coire Bhrochain on the right converge, and you must ski carefully. Soon the ridge widens and there is a good run ENE down to the col below Sron na Lairige. Continue N over the two flat tops of this hill. A magnificent ski-run now goes NNW for 2km, with 400m of descent, down the wide and long snow field in Coire Gorm. This gives either a fast schuss straight down, or a series of wide turns, depending on snow conditions and the skier's skill and tiredness towards the end of a long day.

Before reaching flat ground near Lochan Odhar, traverse NE and ski down towards the Sinclair Memorial Hut. The easiest crossing of the Allt Druidh is about 200 metres upstream from the hut. Then climb again, N then NE along

Cairn Toul from the summit of Braeriach   *D.J. Bennet*

the line of the path through the Chalamain Gap, just E of Creag a' Chalamain. It is quite awkward to ski through the Gap if there is a shortage of snow, in which case it is better to keep higher up the hillside on the SE side of the Gap. This takes you out onto the expansive moor stretching E towards Coire Cas, and inspection will show where the snow cover gives the best route. There is a series of terraces, separated by steeper banks, which often hold snow and allow a gradually descending traverse to be made across the undulating moor and over the streams flowing from Coire an Lochain and Coire an t-Sneachda, with a final level traverse to the Coire Cas car park. If the moor is snow-covered, you will get a long easy run, with fine views south to the cliffs of these two corries and north to the forest of Glen More, which will be greatly appreciated at the end of a long, hard and magnificent day.

Ski run down the Allt a' Choire Mhoir from Ben Macdui to the Lairig Ghru   *D.J. Bennet*

Beinn Mheadhoin above Loch Avon   *I. Peter*

Beinn Mheadhoin; 1182m; (OS Sheet 36; 024017).
Starting point at the car park in Coire Cas (990060); altitude 630m. Distance 15km. Height climbed 1390m. Time 7-8 hours. Rating: ★★★★/IV.

Although less than 6km from the Coire Cas car park on Cairn Gorm, Beinn Mheadhoin is much less accessible than it might appear at first sight, for it is surrounded by deep glens and corries, crags and lochs. Its ascent takes one into one of the wildest and grandest parts of the Cairngorms, and it is an excellent expedition on skis.

From the car park in Coire Cas ascend to the W of the ski tows, up the Fiacaill a' Choire Chais ridge to its top at Pt. 1141m. Continue SSE, skiing easily at first, then more steeply down Coire Raibeirt to the shore of Loch Avon. The best line on the steep lower section of the corrie is usually on the right side of the stream.

If Loch Avon is securely frozen, cross it and climb SE up the steep slopes of a little corrie at whose head a col is reached 400 metres SW of the summit of Beinn Mheadhoin. If the ice on Loch Avon is not safe, follow the shore SW and make a crossing of the headstream at the lowest safe point. Thread hummocky terrain E below the great cliffs of Carn Etchachan, and turn S up the Allt nan Stacan Dubha towards the Loch Etchachan col. Near the col strike E then NE up the broad ridge to Pt. 1163m and continue along the upper plateau with its granite tors or Barns to the summit.

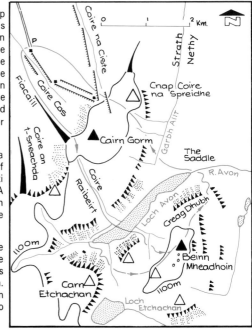

An excellent descent run of 450m goes NNE down a wide snow basin. When this steepens at the outcrops of Creag Dhubh either keep to the right of the rocks or ski down the line of a little stream which penetrates them. A steep run leads down to the foot of Loch Avon, which again should be crossed either over its ice or across the River Avon near the outlet.

From the foot of Loch Avon climb W for 80m to The Saddle, and the NW much more steeply for 330m. The gradient of this ascent eases halfway up, and one reaches the col between Cnap Coire na Spreidhe and Cairn Gorm. The pistes are a short distance W, and a 600m run down them or along the Sron an Aonaich ridge leads back to the car park.

At the summit of Sgor Gaoith, looking towards Braeriach   C.R. Ford

Mullach Clach a' Bhlair; 1019m; (OS Sheets 35, 36 and 43; 883927).
Sgor Gaoith; 1118m; (OS Sheets 36 and 43; 903989).
Starting point at Achlean farm, Glen Feshie (853976); altitude 330m. Distance 24km. Height climbed 940m. Time 8-9 hours. Rating: ★★★/III.

These hills, which lie from north to south on the east side of Glen Feshie, form the western boundary of the Moine Mhor (the great moss), a high plateau approximatley 950m above sea level. They may be climbed individually from Glen Feshie, but are best combined in a traverse which may be done in either direction. However, as the best descents are at the north end, the route is described from south to north. These hills are very featureless, so accurate navigation in mist is essential.

The end of the public road on the E side of Glen Feshie just N of Achlean farm is the starting point for Mullach Clach a' Bhlair. Follow a path ESE, across a deer fence and then SSE on the uphill side of the fence into the remnant of old Caledonian pine forest where there is a bridge across the Allt Fhearnagan. If there is good snow cover low down, the ascent of Mullach Clach a' Bhlair can be made up the ridge on the S side of Coire Garbhlach, and this is the most direct route.

Ski S across the moor to reach the Allt Garbhlach where it issues from the steep-sided corrie. Cross the river and ascend the hillside beyond, climbing parallel to the edge of the forestry plantation at first and then up the steep slopes above to Meall nan Sleac (800m). There is then a short descent to join a bulldozed track where it comes close to the edge of Coire Garbhlach. Continue up the bulldozed track onto the level plateau, then follow a bearing S for 1km to Mullach Clach a' Bhlair.

If there is little or no snow on the lower slopes, an alternative route goes E from the pine wood up the S side of the Allt Fhearnagan (or along the burn if it is snow filled) to the foot of Coire Gorm. Ascend this corrie, which usually holds snow well, SSE to the summit of Meall Dubhag (998m). The route to Mullach Clach a' Bhlair is then SE for 1½km to round the head of Coire Garbhlach and then SSW for 2km to the summit.

From the summit there is an easy schuss NNE to the stream which flows into Coire Garbhlach, followed by a short climb to Pt. 963m and another gentle descent to a wide open stretch of plateau which drains SE to the River Eidart. The summit of Carn Ban Mor (1052m) is 2km N and is reached by a long gradual ascent. The top is towards the N end of the flat summit, but in deep snow or mist it may be difficult to find any cairn.

The descent to the next col on a bearing NNE is only 40m, followed by an ascent of 100m in the same direction along a broad featureless ridge to Sgor Gaoith, the highest point of the traverse. Although the summit has no cairn, it is an unmistakeably sharp promontory on the edge of the cliffs above Loch Einich.

The ski run from the summit will depend on where the snow has drifted in the corries to its W. The most direct descent is down the Coire Gorm a' Chrom-alltain. If the S side of the Allt a' Chrom-alltain is chosen, do not ski down to its confluence with the Allt Ruadh, but cross about ½km higher and traverse NW round the foot of Meall Tionail to a stile over the deer fence below Coire na Cloiche. Continue NW along the line of a path into a pine wood, and

The east face of Sgor Gaoith from the Moine Mhor   *D.J. Bennet*

cross a small stream to reach a rough track. Follow this down above the N bank of the Allt Ruadh to the road in Glen Feshie 4km N of Achlean.

An alternative route down from Sgor Gaoith goes N along the broad ridge, possibly as far as Sgoran Dubh Mor (1111m), and then NW to the headwaters of the Allt a' Mharcaidh. There is often a very fine run down the corrie between Sgoran Dubh Mor and Geal-charn. Ski down the slopes on the W side of the Allt a' Mharcaidh, and as the forest is approached bear left and follow a deer fence down to a crossing of the Allt nan Cuileach. On the other side of this stream reach the top of a forest track and continue steeply down it to join a much wider forest road. This leads W and in a further 2½km the public road in Glen Feshie is reached near Blackmill, 6km N of Achlean.

Monadh Mor; 1113m; (OS Sheet 43; 938942).
Beinn Bhrotain; 1157m; (OS Sheet 43; 954923).
Starting point at Achlean farm, Glen Feshie (853976); altitude 330m. Distance 26km. Height climbed 910m. Time 8-9 hours. Rating: ★★★/III.

This is a lengthy tour across the extensive plateau of the Moine Mhor which often gives good skiing conditions early in the winter and holds snow better than the more exposed high tops.

From Achlean follow the stalker's path E up Coire Fhearnagan to the plateau just S of Carn Ban Mor. The line of ascent is obvious and the path often holds snow well. In lean years the Allt Fhearnagan or the Allt Meall Dubhag will provide a snowy corridor to the plateau long after the snow elsewhere in the corrie has disappeared.

From Carn Ban Mor descend gentle slopes SE to the Allt Sgairnich, but leave this stream where it loses itself in the snow covered knolls W of Loch nan Cnapan. Pass the lochan to the S and after crossing a shallow depression to the E head for any point on the long ridge of Monadh Mor. The route chosen will depend on the build up of snow on the ridge or in the hollows of its W flank. The ridge itself is bouldery, and if wind-blown may not have a good snow cover.

From the summit continue S for just over 1km to another cairn, then ski quite steeply SE to a narrow col at the head of the spectacular Coire Cath nam Fionn. Care is required in bad visibility. Continue SE for 1km, at first up a steep slope, then onto the flatter summit dome of Beinn Bhrotain, where the boulder strewn nature of the hill makes a good snow cover essential for good skiing.

The valley of the Dee now lies before you, stretching away E to Lochnagar, and the long run down to White Bridge may tempt you. However, to return by the way you have come allows you to relish the vastness of the Moine Mhor plateau. From the top of Monadh Mor the right choice of traverse and schuss should take you back to Loch nan Cnapan with the minimum of effort.

The easiest re-ascent from the lochan goes due W to the col between Meall Dubhag and Carn Ban Mor, whence the delightful gully of the Allt Meall Dubhag, which holds snow well in spring, leads down to the Allt Fhearnagan. A steeper run may be had from the shoulder of Carn Ban Mor, skiing into the funnel-shaped gully of the upper Allt Fhearnagan or down the convex slopes of Ciste Mhearad on its S side. Ski on down the Allt Fhearnagan for as far as there is snow; it is not unusual to be able to ski right down to the upper deer fence on a narrow ribbon of snow beside the burn.

The ascent from Glen Feshie to the Moine Mhor near Coire Garbhlach   J. Whitaker

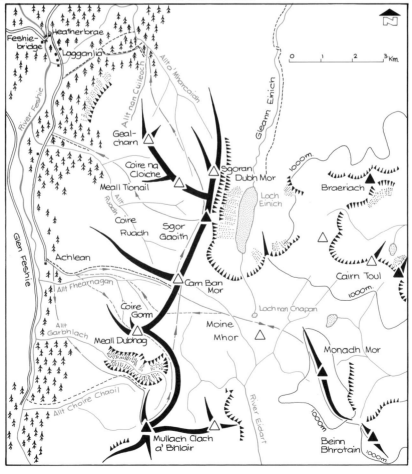

Gleouraich from Spidean Mialach, with Sgurr a' Mhaoraich beyond   D.J. Bennet

Gleouraich; 1035m; (OS Sheet 33; 039054).
Spidean Mialach; 996m; (OS Sheet 33; 066043).
Starting point on the road on the north side of Loch Quoich at (033027); altitude 210m. Distance 13km. Height climbed 1120m. Time 7-8 hours. Rating: ★★★★/IV.

Although these mountains are relatively remote, the effort required to reach them is amply rewarded by an excellent traverse and superb scenery. However, as the route described is technically demanding, with steep ascents to both peaks and a very steep descent, confined by rocks, to the intermediate Fiar Bhealaich, only experienced ski mountaineers should attempt the traverse. A good covering of snow is required before this traverse is feasible on ski.

While the southern slopes are predominantly grassy, providing relatively easy routes of ascent and descent, the traverse of the ridges along the edges of the steep northern corries with superb views to the Glen Shiel hills and the "Rough Bounds" of Knoydart provides one of the finest traverses in the Western Highlands.

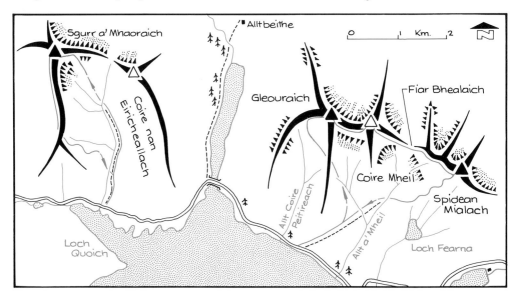

The descent from Spidean Mialach towards Loch Quoich   *D.J. Bennet*

Leave the road above the north shore of Loch Quoich 400m east of the Allt Coire Peitireach where a stalkers' path creates a gap in the rhododendron bushes. Follow this path NE across the hillside, then contour round to the N under a shoulder into Coire Mheil. Continue NW up the stream to level ground S of and below the summit of Gleouraich.

Turn N and climb 100m before traversing NW into upper Coire Peitireach. The ascent N to the ridge W of the summit is very steep, but this section may be avoided by continuing the traverse to the W before ascending to the ridge. Having reached the ridge turn E and ascend steeply at first to the summit of Gleouraich.

From the summit continue E for ½km, descending 70m to a shallow col, then climb 40m to Craig Coire na Fiar Bhealaich. From this top descend E to the Fiar Bhealaich (1006m). Considerable care is required as it is necessary to ski near the edge of the precipitous northern corrie to avoid a band of low cliffs on the SE slopes which is not visible from above.

From the bealach the initial ascent of 200m to the SE is steep and rocky. Thereafter the route is on easier ground following the edge of the northern corries to the summit of Spidean Mialach.

From the summit at first ski down the easy open slopes to the SW aiming for Loch Fearna. After descending 200m bear W and traverse across the slope to Coire Mheil. Given sufficient snow, the lower grassy corrie down to the road may be descended at any point.

Sgurr a' Mhaoraich; 1027m; (OS Sheet 33; 984065).
Starting point on the road on the north side of Loch Quoich at (993036); altitude 210m. Distance 8km. Height climbed 820m. Time 4-5 hours. Rating: ★★★/III.

This isolated mountain to the west of Gleouraich gives a fine ascent on skis which is shorter and easier than the traverse of Gleouraich and Spidean Mialach just described. However, although the skiing may be quite uncomplicated, the position of Sgurr a' Mhaoraich, rising directly above the head of Loch Hourn, makes it a superb viewpoint, and no other ski tour described in this book gives (on a clear day) such views of the western sea lochs and mountains.

The ascent goes up the stalker's path in Coire nan Eiricheallach, skiing easily N then NW up to the head of the corrie where the slope steepens under the E ridge of Sgurr a' Mhaoraich. Before reaching this ridge, below the rocks of its crest where a huge square boulder is a useful landmark, bear up to the left (W) on a rising traverse to reach the E ridge above its rocky part at about 900m, where the crest is quite broad. The steep rise above this point can be avoided by a rising traverse left leading onto the upper slopes of the S ridge which are broad and easy angled, and rise directly to the summit.

The descent may be made by the same route. Alternatively, one may ski down the S ridge, but its upper part has many knolls and rocky outcrops, and a good snow cover is needed. In good conditions, however, this ridge gives very interesting skiing down to about 650m, at which height one should bear SE down towards the lower part of Coire nan Eiricheallach.

On the ridge from Carn Ghluasaid to Sgurr nan Conbhairean, looking west to A'Chralaig   D.J. Bennet

Carn Ghluasaid; 957m; (OS Sheet 34; 146125).
Sgurr nan Conbhairean; 1110m; (OS Sheet 34; 130139).
A'Chralaig; 1120m; (OS Sheet 34; 094148).
Starting point on the A87 road on the north side of Loch Cluanie at the foot of Coire Lair (130104); altitude 230m. Distance 18km. Height climbed 1370m. Time 7-8 hours. Rating: ★★★★/III.

On the north side of Loch Cluanie at the head of Glen Moriston there is a high range of mountains culminating in A'Chralaig. Their traverse is a very fine ski expedition which fully rewards the long journey from the south to reach them, and there is a great pleasure in skiing in this part of the Highlands, surrounded by so many other superb peaks in an area not much frequented by skiers. The quality of the traverse lies partly in this mountain setting, partly in the character of the peaks, ridges and corries, and partly in the skiing itself which, although not unduly difficult, is very varied and interesting. However, there are two or three sections where careful navigation and skiing are required in bad weather.

Leave the road at a convenient parking place just E of the Allt Coire Lair and climb N up easy slopes on the E side of the burn. After 1½km bear NE up the N side of the stream which flows down from the plateau of Carn Ghluasaid, and continue easily to this summit where the most prominent cairn (which is not quite on the highest point of the plateau) overlooks the wild corries at the head of the River Doe.

Ski W down a broad smooth ridge, dropping only 60m to a col from which an easy climb of 100m leads to Creag a' Chaorainn (999m). The ridge turns W for a short distance and drops barely 20m before climbing much more steeply in a NNW direction to Sgurr nan Conbhairean. The entire ridge from Carn Ghluasaid to Sgurr nan Conbhairea is very smooth (the underlying terrain being grass and moss), as are the slopes on its S side dropping into Coire Lair. The N side of the ridge is precipitous and liable to be corniced.

Ski SW from the summit of Sgurr nan Conbhairean down a wide slope which steepens and converges to a little col. At that point the ridge is narrow, with steep drops on both sides, and beyond it rises again very gradually (skins not needed) for about 200 metres to the top of Drochaid an Tuill Easaich (1000m). There the ridge turns NW and drops, gradually at first and then much more steeply, to the Bealach Choire a' Chait (c. 730m). One can ski along the crest of the ridge quite easily to the steepening, and then take to the SW flank for a descending traverse towards the bealach. If there is a good snow cover, this descent gives a very good run, otherwise the ridge and its SW flank may be punctuated by rocks and boulders.

The Bealach Choire a' Chait is a wide flat col, and anyone wanting to shorten the traverse can do so by skiing very easily S down the corrie. The ridge to A' Chralaig, however, rises directly from the col, steeply at first, then at an easier angle until the final steepening leads to the main crest of the mountain ¾km SE of the summit. The final climb up this broad ridge takes one above the surrounding peaks to the large and splendidly built cairn of A' Chralaig.

Sgurr nan Conbhairean from the east ridge of A'Chralaig   *D.J. Bennet*

Ski back down the SE ridge to the junction of the S and E ridges. If there is good snow cover, continue skiing down the S ridge for a further 1km, then turn E into Coire a' Chait. If there is a poor snow cover on this ridge, it may be better to retrace the ascent route along the E ridge, skiing steeply down it for a short distance before turning SE and running down into the wide open spaces of Coire a' Chait. Both these routes converge in the lower part of the corrie, and given a good snow cover there is plenty more interesting skiing down towards Loch Cluanie. Altogether the run from A' Chralaig to the Loch Cluanie road gives over 4km of very varied and enjoyable skiing with a descent of almost 900m if there is snow down to the loch. It is a fitting end to a grand traverse.

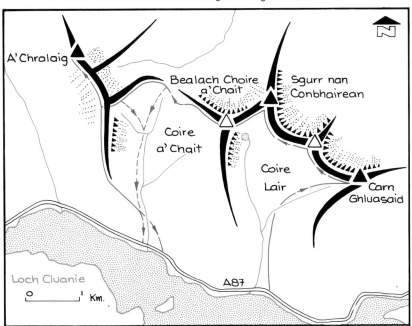

Skiing west from Toll Creagach towards Tom a' Choinich   D. Snadden

Toll Creagach; 1054m; (OS Sheet 25; 194283).
Tom a' Choinich; 1111m; (OS Sheet 25; 163273).
Starting point on the road up Glen Affric from Cannich to Affric Lodge, 3km ENE of Affric Lodge at (216242); altitude 230m. Distance 15km. Height climbed 1100m. Time 5-6 hours. Rating: ★★★/IV. (For Toll Creagach alone: Distance 12km. Height climbed 820m. Time 4 hours).

These two mountains give good skiing, with reliable snow cover often until late in spring. The east face of Tom a' Choinich in particular holds snow well. They can be climbed separately, or combined in an excellent traverse. Toll Creagach gives good skiing on its easy-angled slopes, while Tom a' Choinich, in marked contrast, gives some challenging runs on its steep east face, which should only be attempted by competent skiers who are happy on steep and possibly dangerous slopes.

Start at the point where the road up Glen Affric crosses the Abhainn Gleann nam Fiadh near the W end of Loch Beinn a' Mheadhoin, where there is a convenient parking place. Follow a track E then N for 2km up Gleann nam Fiadh, then go NE into a side glen. Cross the level floor of this glen to reach the slopes between Beinn Eun and the Allt Coire an t-Sneachda. These slopes can be climbed almost anywhere, giving access to the vast snowy expanse of Coire an t-Sneachda, up which there is a long tedious plod with little in the way of views. From the corrie it is easy to gain the S or E ridges, and these lead directly to the summit of Toll Creagach, where the reward for the laborious ascent may well be magnificent views to the north and west. If you are not going on to Tom a' Choinich, the shortest run back to the road is by the ascent route.

From the summit cairn a line of widely spaced fence posts leads W down broad slopes to the shallow col before the lower West Top (952m). From this col there is a good run S down the Allt a' Choire Odhair, and for those with plenty of time and energy the slopes to the NNW give an excellent ski run down towards the Allt Lub nam Meann, but this is a long detour on the way to Tom a' Choinich, adding at least an hour to the day. The best option is to put on skins for the short ascent to the West Top. From

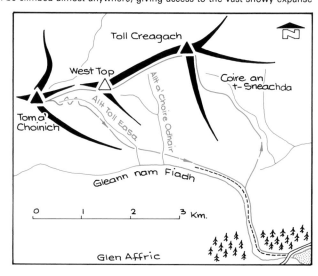

there the descent to the col below Tom a' Choinich can be made by skiing down the W ridge, but this ridge is rather rocky and should only be skied if there is a good snow cover. A better alternative may well be to ski down a shallow open gully on the S side of the W ridge, and so reach the Bealach Toll Easa (873m).

The climb from the bealach up the E ridge of Tom a' Choinich on skis is very pleasant and poses no difficulties for the first part. The final section is steep and narrow, and the last 50-100m may have to be climbed on foot. The summit of Tom a' Choinich is a marvellous one, with steep slopes dropping on all sides and other large mountains all round. The E face is over 1km long and gives several possible ski descents, but the whole face is likely to be corniced and the first 50m of any descent is exceedingly steep, possibly in excess of 40°. It is usually possible to breach the line of cornices at the point where the E ridge joins the summit plateau near the cairn. The sudden transition from the horizontal summit to the apparent verticality of the descent slopes is quite dramatic, and the serious nature of the descent should not be underestimated as the headwall can pose an avalanche risk in certain conditions.

Once the initial slope has been safely negotiated, excellent skiing can be had right down the Toll Easa to the floor of Gleann nam Fiadh, where the way along the stalker's track back to the road in Glen Affric is obvious.

Creag Dubh; 946m; (OS Sheet 25; 200351).
Carn nan Gobhar; 992m; (OS Sheet 25; 182344).
Starting point at the end of the public road up Glen Cannich at the Loch Mullardoch dam (219316); altitude 250m. Distance 12km. Height climbed 860m. Time 5-6 hours. Rating: ★★/II.

This is the nearest mountain group to the road end at Loch Mullardoch in Glen Cannich. Like many ideal ski mountains, they have rounded contours and smooth slopes, and a tour of the broad ridges encircling Coire an t-Sith gives a pleasant short excursion of no difficulty. This corrie holds snow well and usually gives some good skiing even in years of lean snow cover.

From the dam a path goes along the N side of the loch, and it is followed W as far as the Allt Mullardoch. From there a faint path branches off and heads N up the E bank of the burn, leading in 1¼km to the crossing of another small burn. It is quite possible to continue up Coire an t-Sith and make a direct and easy ascent of the S face of Creag Dubh, however a rising traverse across the lower slopes of the W ridge of Pt.861m gives access to several steep tongues of snow. The ascent of any one of these is worthwhile as the gloomy recesses of the corrie are soon left behind, but this route should only be attempted if the snow cover is good.

Once on the crest of the ridge climb ENE until a level traverse N can be made over Pt.814m, and then NW across a shallow col, where a dry stone dyke is a useful landmark in thick weather. The ascent to Creag Dubh from the col is simple, though the summit plateau tends to be rocky if there is poor snow cover.

Equally easy is the traverse to Carn nan Gobhar where the true summit is a small pile of stones 200 metres N of the more obvious cairn. There are two possible descents. One goes back to the col towards Creag Dubh and then SSE straight down to Coire an t-Sith, but the slope should be treated with care as windslab is not uncommon at its top. Alternatively a safer route which gives good skiing but requires better snow cover goes down the SSE ridge of Carn nan Gobhar to the col below Mullach na Maoile. From there ski down into Coire an t-Sith and rejoin the path back to the lochside.

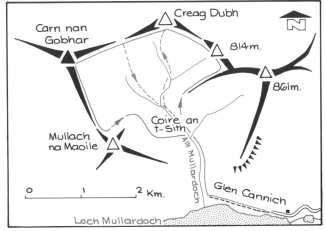

Looking south from the summit of Sgurr na Lapaich   *D. Snadden*

Sgurr na Lapaich; 1150m; (OS Sheet 25; 161351).
An Riabhachan; 1129m; (OS Sheet 25; 134345).
Starting point at the power station in Gleann Innis an Loichel at the end of the road up Glen Strathfarrar (183381); altitude 200m. Distance 14km. Height climbed 1290m. Time 6-7 hours. Rating: ★★★★/III.

Sgurr na Lapaich is one of the finest mountains at the head of the long glens that penetrate westward from Strath Glass, and its pointed summit and eastern corries can be glimpsed as one approaches the mountains up the strath. To its west An Riabhachan is a long level ridge right in the heart of the wilderness between Loch Mullardoch and Loch Monar. To ski across these two mountains in the depth of winter is to experience in no uncertain way the isolation and grandeur of this remote part of the Highlands.

Sgurr na Lapaich can be climbed on ski from Loch Mullardoch either by itself or in combination with Carn nan Gobhar, whose ascent is described on the preceding page. However the approach along the shores of the loch is tedious, and the traverse from Carn nan Gobhar involves an ascent of the rugged and precipitous E face of Sgurr na Lapaich which, though quite possible, involves carrying skis up the steepest part. The approach from the head of Glen Strathfarrar is better, and the ascent from there combined with a traverse to An Riabhachan gives an excellent expedition into this wild country.

The approach up Glen Strathfarrar is along a private road guarded by a locked gate near Struy in Strath Glass. Access through this gate can usually be arranged by contacting the gatekeeper in advance. (Telephone 0463 76 260). It should be borne in mind that the road may be impassable due to snow.

The climb starts at the small power station in Gleann Innis an Loichel, reached by driving across the Loch Monar dam and continuing a few kilometres to the end of the road. Proceed W along a rough track for 1km to a small wooden bridge over the Uisge Misgeach, and follow the track for 200 metres further to its end. Continue SW beside a burn for 400 metres then turn S and climb the steep slopes above to a large depression on the N side of Sgurr na Lapaich. This depression holds snow well and gives an easy, though fairly long, ascent to the crest of the NE ridge. From there the ridge is followed in a graceful sweep over a small subsidiary top and up a steepening corniced section to the summit.

Descend due S from the summit of Sgurr na Lapaich for ½km to a col 110m lower, being very careful in bad visibility as the slopes to the E are corniced. From there a broad gully gives excellent skiing down to the col at the foot of the SW ridge, and if one does not want to go further it is possible to descend N from this col to Loch Mor. The slopes are steep at first, but should pose no difficulty, and from the loch the return to the glen is easy.

The direct ascent of An Riabhachan from the col goes up the E ridge, which is not steep but becomes narrow and exposed in its upper part. An easier alternative is to traverse SW from the col across An Garbh-choire to reach the SE ridge and climb it. Both these ridges end at the E top, from where an easy traverse leads along the level summit ridge to the highest point.

Skiing down the south-west ridge of Sgurr na Lapaich towards An Riabhachan   D. Snadden

Two descents are possible. The first is to return to the E top and descend the SE ridge, traversing An Garbh-choire to the col between An Riabhachan and Sgurr na Lapaich, thus joining the alternative descent route mentioned above. It is important not to leave the SE ridge too soon as the upper part is corniced on its NE side overlooking An Garbh-choire. The second descent requires good snow cover, but is better in that in takes one into the remote and bleak country on the N side of An Riabhachan, and in good conditions gives a long and uninterrupted run back to the glen. Ski NE from the summit by a descending traverse, then a steeper downhill run to a little shallow plateau level with the lowest cliffs above Loch Beag. Descend N of these cliffs to reach the level corrie N of Loch Beag. From there the best route down to the glen will be dictated by prevailing snow conditions, but avoid following the Allt an Eas Bhain Mhoir as it flows down a steep gorge. A long descending traverse across the lower slopes of Sgurr na Lapaich may well give the most continuous skiing.

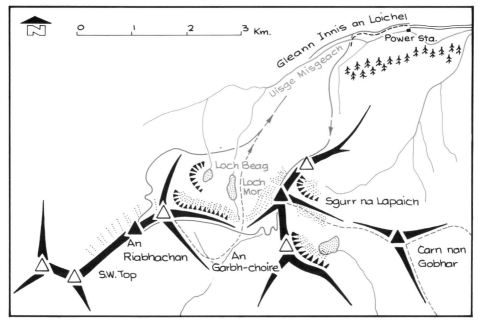

The North Glen Strathfarrar Ridge from Sgurr na Lapaich

D. Snadden

Sgurr Fhuar-thuill; 1049m; (OS Sheet 25; 235437).
Sgurr a' Choire Ghlais; 1083m; (OS Sheet 25; 259430).
Carn nan Gobhar; 992m; (OS Sheet 25; 273439).
Sgurr na Ruaidhe; 993m; (OS Sheet 25; 289426).
Starting point in Glen Strathfarrar at the foot of the Allt Toll a'Mhuic (224392); altitude 160m.
Distance 17km. Height climbed 1550m. Time 6-7 hours. Rating: ★★★★/III.

The high mountain range on the north side of Glen Strathfarrar gives a magnificent ski tour in a wild and lonely setting, crossing four Munros and two Tops. The traverse is described from west to east as this should give the best descents on skis. The approach is along the private road in Glen Strathfarrar, and access up this road is barred by a locked gate near Struy (394406). In winter advance arrangements for access need to be made with the gatekeeper (Telephone 0463 76 260).

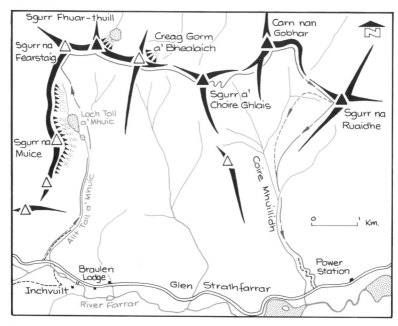

It is a real advantage to have two cars for this trip as the finishing point is 6km along the road from the starting point. One car should be left at the foot of Coire Mhuillidh (284386), and the other one taken to the starting point at the foot of the Allt Toll a' Mhuic. From there climb NE up a Landrover track for 1km and continue along the line of the stalker's path to Loch Toll a' Mhuic. Ascend fairly steep slopes N of the loch until at about 800m the floor of the corrie becomes more level just below the steep SE face of Sgurr na Fearstaig (1015m). This face can pose an avalanche risk and should be avoided by a short steep climb W to reach the S ridge of Sgurr na Fearstaig, which is easily reached up this ridge.

The next section to Sgurr Fhuar-thuill is very straightforward, the descent being short enough to hardly warrant the removal of skins. From its summit ski SE down the ridge to the next col, taking care to avoid the precipitous and often corniced slopes to the N. The ascent to Creag Ghorm a' Bhealaich (1030m) by its W ridge should pose no difficulty, but the skiing along this quite narrow section of the ridge is very enjoyable.

In poor visibility the next section of the ridge can be the trickiest of the traverse, as the slopes on both sides are very steep and large cornices can form on the N side. Ski S from the summit at first, gradually veering E to reach the narrow col at the foot of the WNW ridge of Sgurr a' Choire Ghlais. The ascent of this ridge to the summit of the highest peak of the traverse should cause no undue difficulty, although the upper part is quite steep. On a good day the views from this point are truly magnificent.

The next objective is the col between Sgurr a' Choire Ghlais and Carn nan Gobhar. The best descent is to ski steeply down the E flank of Sgurr a' Choire Ghlais and, before getting too low, traverse NE to the col. From there a short ascent E leads to the flat plateau of Carn nan Gobhar, whose summit is ½km NE. At this point on the traverse the character of the mountains changes quite dramatically, for until now the peaks have been rocky and steep and the ridges narrow, but from here the contours are gentler, the ridges broader, the mountains much less rugged and the summits further apart.

From Carn nan Gobhar ski E for about ½km, then S to the next col. From there the summit of Sgurr na Ruaidhe is easily reached by its broad smooth NE ridge. In good conditions there are many fine descents from this hill, the most direct being down the shallow corrie SW. This gives a fine run into Coire Mhuillidh. In conditions of poor snow cover, the gully which drops WNW from the summit may give a more reliable descent to the corrie. Finally, a long easy-angled run S, always keeping on the E side of the Allt Coire Mhuillidh, leads down to the road in Glen Strathfarrar.

Beinn a' Bha'ach Ard; 862m; (OS Sheet 26; 361435)
Starting point ¾km west of Struy Bridge on the A831 road in Strathglass at (395406); altitude 60m. Distance 12km. Height climbed 850m. Time 4 hours. Rating: ★★/II.

The eye of anyone driving westwards along the road on the south side of the Beauly Firth is invariably drawn to the shapely peak of Beinn a' Bha'ach Ard. With a height of 862m it is not a high mountain, but it is accessible and gives an excellent short tour. If there is a lot of snow on the roads in Strathglass and the glens which radiate from it, then this hill may well give the only accessible ski tour in the area. It is best climbed when snow cover is low, and being in the weather shadow of the big ranges to the west, it often gives a good day when these big mountains are stormbound and inaccessible.

Fifty metres before the locked gate at the foot of Glen Strathfarrar there is a rough track which winds its way N through a small forest. Follow this track past the tree-line, then head towards Loch na Beiste. From there climb gentle slopes NW, going first to Sgurr a' Phollain to enjoy the short easy traverse from there to Beinn a' Bha'ach Ard. This traverse presents no difficulties until the last few metres before the summit cairn is reached, where the going is somewhat steep and rocky.

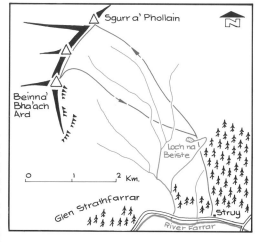

This isolated little summit is a splendid vantage point, and commands unobstructed views of the Moray Firth and its associated coastline. For the bold the drop off the summit to the SE provides a short, but steep and exciting descent to the gentler slopes below. Others would be better advised to return to the small col NE of the summit and reach these same slopes by a less steep descent. Further down, the hillside can be skied virtually anywhere, though you should aim eventually to reach Loch na Beiste in order to reverse the ascent route used earlier.

Sgurr nan Clach Geala from Carn na Criche   *D. Snadden*

Meall a' Chrasgaidh; 934m; (OS Sheet 20; 184733).
Sgurr Mor; 1110m; (OS Sheet 20; 203718).
Beinn Liath Mhor Fannaich; 954m; (OS Sheet 20; 219724).
Starting point at Lochdrum, west end of Loch Droma, on the A835 road, (253755); altitude 270m.
Distance 17km. Height climbed 1140m. Time 7-9 hours. Rating: ★★★★/IV.

The traverse on skis of the three central peaks of the Fannaichs is a long and serious expedition, not least because of the remoteness of these mountains. Technically, the hardest part of the traverse is the ascent and descent of Sgurr Mor, a fine steep peak whose slopes if icy will call for ice axe and crampons. The approach goes for several kilometres over rough moorland which, if not snow covered, will entail a tedious walk in and out, so a good snow cover down the road is a great advantage.

Cross the dam at the W end of Loch Droma and follow the track W beside a large concrete pipe. Cross the Allt a'Mhadaidh and continue up its N side along the track to its end 1½km further. Ahead the grandeur of the big corries and the peak of Sgurr Mor gradually unfolds. Continue beyond the end of the track along the Allt a'Mhadaidh where the going is rough unless there is a good cover of snow, and reach Loch a'Mhadaidh in a wonderful setting, silent under the foreboding cliffs of Carn na Criche.

From the loch there are two possibilities for the ascent to Meall a' Chrasgaidh. The more obvious and easier is to skirt round the N shore of the loch and climb the straightforward but quite steep snow slopes leading to the col between it and Carn na Criche. The other route is more interesting and aesthetically pleasing as it leads directly to the summit. Climb NW from the loch onto the crest of Creag Raineach Mor, the level lower part of the NE ridge of Meall a' Chrasgaidh, and ascend this ridge until progress on skis is halted by a steepening. The final 200m is a delightful climb, carrying skis, up snow and rocks which are quite exposed but not difficult. Ice axe and possibly crampons also will be needed.

The run SE from the summit of Meall a'Chrasgaidh gives enjoyable skiing down a broad smooth ridge to the col at 820m below Carn na Criche. There is an easy descent NE from this col to Loch a' Mhadaidh, but once the col is passed there is no safe descent on the N side of the ridge until Beinn Liath Mhor Fannaich is reached. Climb easily to the summit of Carn na Criche (961m) from where the best views along the corniced ridge to Sgurr nan Clach Geala are obtained. There is a very short descent SE to the col at the foot of Sgurr Mor. The slopes which drop NE from this col are deceptive as there is an unseen cliff half way down.

The ascent of Sgurr Mor on skis from the col can be problematical, and in icy conditions unjustifiable. The ridge rising directly to the summit is steep and rocky, and the only feasible ski route is up its E side which is also steep and very exposed, and should only be tackled with caution. The safest option is probably to climb the ridge on foot. The summit of Sgurr Mor is an impressive and, in winter, a lonely place; on all sides the snow or ice covered slopes fall steeply to glens and corries far below, and the skier is acutely aware that the most demanding ski run of the day lies ahead.

Looking towards Sgurr Mor from the ridge to Beinn Liath Mhor Fannaich   *D. Snadden*

From the summit set off in a southerly direction and ski down the ridge for about 200 metres. If the snow cover is thin the eroded character of the slope, forming a series of terraces with short steep drops between them, will give some disconcertingly bumpy skiing. At this point the ridge to Beinn Liath Mhor Fannaich turns off E, still dropping steeply. In poor visibility this ridge can be difficult to find, and meticulous navigation is required as the drop on the N side of the crest is precipitous and the edge usually corniced, and on the S side the slope is steep also. A little lower down the angle eases and the ridge becomes broader and gives a magnificent ski run over a small rise and on to Beinn Liath Mhor Fannaich where the last climb of the day is agreeably short.

Ski NE off the summit into the northernmost of the two corries on the E side of Beinn Liath Mhor Fannaich. The initial run off the summit is steep but lower down there is good skiing on easier slopes. Two-thirds of the way down the corrie make a descending traverse N under the terminal crags of the NE ridge to reach the watershed at the NW end of Loch Sgeireach. Continue an easy descent N to reach the track by the Allt a' Mhadaidh, with Loch Droma only a short distance away.

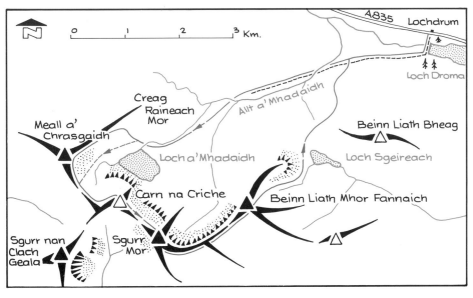

Skiing north-west from Am Faochagach towards Loch Prille and Cona'Mheall   D. Snadden

Am Faochagach; 954m;(OS Sheet 20; 304794).
Cona 'Mheall; 980m; (OS Sheet 20; 275816).
Beinn Dearg; 1084m; (OS Sheet 20; 259812).
Starting point on the A835 road at the bridge over the Abhainn an Torrain Dubh (277743) near the north-west end of Loch Glascarnoch; altitude 260m. Distance 22km. Height climbed 1430m. Time 8-9 hours. Rating: ★★★★/IV.

This is a magnificent ski-mountaineering expedition, seldom undertaken, over remote and rugged mountains. However, for anyone lucky enough to do it in good conditions, it is certain to give a memorable day. Am Faochagach is a fine ski mountain in its own right and gives a variety of excellent ascents and descents. Combining its ascent with a traverse of Cona 'Mheall and Beinn Dearg gives a long and demanding tour which should only be attempted by experienced, fit and reasonably fast parties. Good snow cover is essential for this trip, and the snow line should preferably be low enough to allow skiing from the roadside, otherwise the walk across the rough moor at the NW end of Loch Glascarnoch is tiresome.

Set off from the A835 road in a NE direction towards the Abhainn a' Garbhrain. This river can pose crossing difficulties in summer, but in the grip of a hard winter it is usually reduced to a trickle. A straightforward climb up slopes to the NE brings you without difficulty to the long ridge which winds its way up to the summit of Am Faochagach. The long haul up to the top is well compensated by the superb sight of Choire Ghranda, which nestles between Cona 'Mheall and Beinn Dearg.

From the summit of Am Faochagach you will be struck by the dramatic contrast between the gently rolling slopes that drop away NE to Glen Beag and the wild mountain architecture of Cona 'Mheall to the NW. Here it is time to pause, for if it has taken more than 3 hours to reach this summit, you will not complete the trip in the time given and it might be advisable to return. If you chose to go on you will be rewarded with a long and easy descent to Loch Prille, traversing either side of the knoll of Meallan Ban. The feeling of isolation on this descent is complete, and at its end Loch Prille provides a truly remote setting for an early lunch.

This is the place to contemplate the long climb to Cona 'Mheall, for once you have embarked on it there is no way back to your car without completing the traverse of Beinn Dearg. It is possible to by-pass Cona 'Mheall by ascending the glen to Loch Tuath and then climbing onto the plateau between Beinn Dearg and Meall nan Ceapraichean, however it is probably just as quick and certainly a finer route to ascend the E ridge of Cona 'Mheall. This is a long and fairly steep ascent of 450m and good snow is needed to cover the rocky ridge. It is possible to climb on skis without too much difficulty to within 30m of the summit, where the final steepening will probably have to be tackled on foot, and may require crampons.

The descent NW from Cona 'Mheall is quite straightforward, though care is required in bad visibility to avoid steep slopes to the NE and SW. From the col at the foot of this descent a short climb W leads to a dry-stone dyke

*A steep climb up the east ridge of
Cona'Mheall*   *D. Snadden*

which points the way up the NE ridge of
Beinn Dearg. The ridge itself is rocky and
the best ascent route lies on the exposed
slopes E of the dyke. These slopes are not
too steep and should present no difficulty
except in very icy conditions. Near the
summit plateau the dyke turns W and the
cairn on Beinn Dearg is 200 metres S of
this point.

You are now about to embark on one of
the finest downhill runs in the district, one
to be savoured, for the mountain and the
view are magnificent. From the summit ski
SSW down into the snowy bowl between
the S and SW ridges, and ski on along the
line of the burn in the shallow corrie lower
down to reach the Allt Mhucarnaich. The
descent to this point is over 600m, and
gives 2km of fine skiing. Continue SE along
the Allt 'a Garbhrain where the slope is just
enough to keep the skis running for 4km to
Loch Garbhrain, though some poling will
be required. At the loch it is worth putting
on skins for the last time to traverse the
final tedious slopes back to the road.

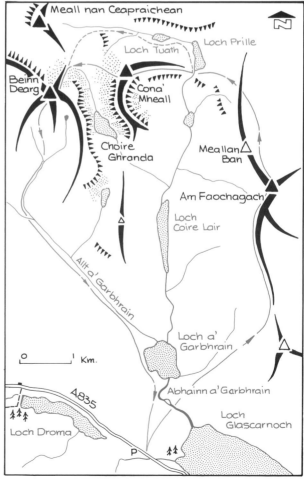

On the summit ridge of Ben Wyvis   *D. Snadden*

Ben Wyvis; 1046m; (OS Sheet 20; 463684).
Starting point at Garbat (412678) on the A835 road from Dingwall to Ullapool; altitude 150m.
Distance 17km. Height climbed 1000m. Time 6-7 hours. Rating: ★★★/II.

The massive bulk of Ben Wyvis ranks as one of the most important ski mountains in the Northern Highlands.
There have been plans to build a mountain railway on the southern flank and develop a ski resort on the mountain,
but these plans are at present in abeyance. For the ski-mountaineer there are many possible routes, all with quite
long approaches, most are technically easy and the views on a clear day are unsurpassed.

The western approach from the A835 road is the shortest, and will be described below. Another very long and
fine approach may be made from the south, starting at Heights of Keppoch (reached from the A834 road between
Dingwall and Strathpeffer) and crossing the long rising moor towards the eastern corries of Ben Wyvis. These
corries, Coire na Feola and Choire Mhor, give some exhilarating mountain skiing, best in spring when the snow
conditions are stable. Once on the summit ridge of Ben Wyvis the skiing is superb, for the terrain is smooth and a
good cover of snow turns the grassy corries into vast snow bowls.

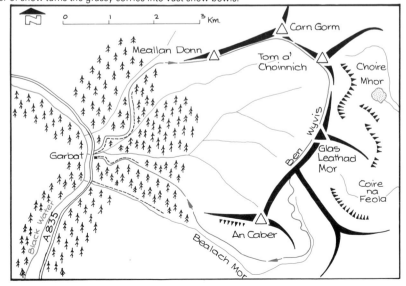

For the western approach start at Garbat, where cars can be parked opposite the farm. Walk a short distance N across the Allt a' Gharbh Bhaid bridge, and then follow a forest track NW into the Garbat Forest. The track is followed to its end at a large fire-break, then follow a smaller fire-break NE until the edge of the forest is reached. Continue along the edge of the forest and head E towards Meallan Donn. There is a deer fence about ½km above the forest with a gate in it near the crest of Meallan Donn. From that point ski up the ridge to join the main ridge of Ben Wyvis between Carn Gorm and Tom a' Choinnich. Finally climb steeply in zig-zags up the NW ridge of this Top.

From Tom a' Choinnich ski first SE then SSW down easy-angled slopes to the col below the highest summit of Ben Wyvis – Glas Leathad Mor. The ascent to it from the col is up a broad ridge. The magnificent view from the summit on a clear day should be savoured before setting off SW along the broad and level ridge. On a day of storm and bad visibility, however, one's attention should be concentrated on accurate navigation along the featureless ridge.

One kilometre SW of the summit one reaches the junction of the main ridge leading on to An Caber and a nameless ridge branching out SE above Coire na Feola. Between these two ridges there is a wide south-facing corrie which may well be a vast snowfield. This corrie gives a superb descent, following the curving course of the Allt a' Bhealaich Mhoir, down to the level, narrow defile of the Bealach Mor. Once through this pass, where some poling may be needed to maintain one's momentum, bear N away from the stream to reach the forest fence at a gate leading to a fire-break. Follow this down through the forest to the road at Garbat.

The great NW flank of Ben Wyvis forms a long concave slope 600m high from the summit ridge down to the upper edge of the Garbat Forest. It presents an obvious challenge to the adventurous skier, but there is a considerable avalanche risk, and one of the very few ski-mountaineering fatal accidents in Scotland has occurred on this slope. It should thus be attempted only by expert skiers in very good conditions.

Moruisg; 928m; (OS Sheet 25; 101499).
Sgurr nan Ceannaichean; 915m; (OS Sheet 25; 087481).
Starting point in Glen Carron on the A890 road at (082521); altitude 150m. Distance 11km. Height climbed 980m. Time 4-5 hours. Rating: ★★★/III.

This mountain group can be approached either from the north or the south. The southern slopes are reasonably easy, but the approach to them is rather long and circuitous along the track from Craig in Glen Carron to Glenuaig Lodge up the glen of the Allt a' Chonais. By contrast, the northern flanks are much more accessible from Glen Carron, and the slopes are steeper, offering more challenging skiing. This approach from the north is described.

Leave the A890 road through Glen Carron about 1km W of the W end of Loch Sgamhain and cross the nearby footbridge over the River Carron. Cross the railway and then head SE directly up the slopes to Moruisg. These are gentle and uninteresting at first, but they soon steepen dramatically, and care must be taken in choosing a suitable route between the gullies that fall from the summit plateau. A less direct, but easier ascent can be made by traversing E up these slopes to join the N ridge which leads easily to the summit.

On a good day the hills of Torridon, Letterewe and Achnashellach are seen to good advantage from Moruisg. From the summit ski SSW past Pt. 854m to the col below Sgurr nan Ceannaichean. The last part of this descent may be a little rocky, but with good route selection it should be possible to get a continous run from Moruisg to the col.

On this descent the steep and often corniced crags on one's right which drop into Coire Toll nam Bian should be avoided; there is no safe route down into this corrie on skis.

By comparison with its rounded neighbour, Sgurr nan Ceannaichean is an interesting and complex mountain. From the col ascend a short ridge W to join the N ridge of the mountain, and follow it to the summit, a small plateau with the highest cairn at its SE edge. This ascent should not cause difficulty in reasonable conditions, however the steep final section might be awkward if icy.

The descent route is down the shallow NW corrie of Sgurr nan Ceannaichean, but a direct run into the corrie from the summit is not possible because of steep rocks high up. Initially one should ski down either the N or W ridge before traversing into the corrie. In poor visibility the route finding here is very tricky. The easiest option is to ski down the W ridge for ½km where, at an altitude of about 770m, its crest becomes level. (Do not go further down this ridge, as it ends above the very steep W face). Leave the ridge and ski NE on a descending traverse into the corrie, keeping above the two streams (forming a Y) which flow into steep-sided gullies lower down towards Coire an t-Seilich. Once on the E side of these streams, ski N down the broad slope towards the lower part of Coire an t-Seilich, and finally cross the Alltan na Feola and the level moor beyond it to reach the day's starting point.

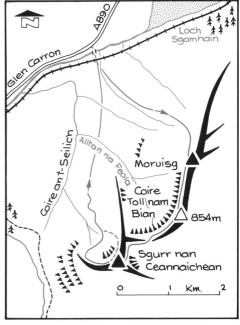

Moruisg from Sgurr nan Ceannaichean, with Fionn Bheinn to the left   *D. Snadden*

Fionn Bheinn; 933m; (OS Sheets 20 and 25; 147621).
Starting point at Achnasheen on the A832 road (162585); altitude 150m. Distance 9km. Height climbed 800m. Time 3-4 hours. Rating: ★★/II.

This featureless hill is a rather tedious climb in summer, however its grassy slopes and rounded contours mean that it is well suited as a ski mountain. It is easily climbed from Achnasheen in a few hours, and can be regarded as no more than a half day tour.

It is usually possible to park beside the school at Achnasheen. From there cross a field towards the obvious gash in the hillside that marks the line of the Allt Achadh na Sine. A steady climb up either side of this stream leads to a small featureless plateau. The most interesting way from this point is to ascend the broad ridge which runs up to Creagan nan Laogh. This is a small subsidiary spur 1km S of the E top of Fionn Bheinn. From there it is a simple matter to cross a broad col and climb directly up to the E top.

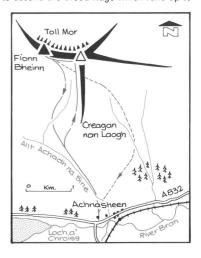

This top overlooks the Toll Mor, and this wild corrie is one of the few redeeming features of Fionn Bheinn. The traverse round the rim of Toll Mor is easy, though in poor visibility care must be taken not to ski too near the cornices on the N side of the ridge.

The main summit of this isolated mountain is a fine viewpoint, with the Fannaichs and Letterewe mountains being well seen. Two descents are possible, the first is to ski SE from the summit, then S to rejoin the ascent route at the small plateau mentioned above. Alternatively, one can ski SE from the summit to the Creagan nan Laogh spur, cross it and continue down the Allt Coire nan Laogh until a traverse back to the day's starting point is possible.Both these routes hold snow well and should give good skiing, and the choice will depend on prevailing snow conditions.

Coire an t-Sneachda, a training ground for extreme skiers   *D.J. Bennet*

Few skiers can resist the challenge of skiing near the limit of their ability, and steep and difficult slopes need not be the preserve of off-piste downhill skiers at fashionable alpine resorts. Such sport can readily be enjoyed in the Scottish Highlands, either for its own sake or as part of an extended tour. For example, in the Cairngorms three or four descents of grade I gullies in Coire an t-Sneachda can be accomplished in a day given good conditions. Alternatively, one might link Lurcher's South Gully, West Gully in Coire Bhrochain of Braeriach, Angel's Ridge and The Couloir in Coire an Lochain to make a very fine and exciting ski tour.

This concluding chapter deals with the equipment, techniques and various problems associated with skiing down steep terrain, and looks at some of the possibilities in the Scottish mountains.

Equipment

Many skiers prefer to use downhill equipment for its strength and reliability in descent. Bindings should have strong springs, well screwed up, as any release on a steep slope is a guarantee of disaster. The skier must retain his skis to have a chance of controlling any mishap. A lifting plate can be fitted to downhill bindings to adapt them for uphill use.

Given a good snow cover, downhill boots with adjustable forward flex can be worn all day with reasonable comfort. If one has to do much walking, light walking boots can be carried for this purpose. Step-in crampons are ideal for use with ski boots, and with them grade I or II gullies should present no problems to a competent climber.

Ski mountaineering boots are variable in comfort and support. Comfort is essential, and the boot should be able to positively grip and support the ankle and lower leg in the normal knee forward position. Ski mountaineering bindings are also variable, particularly in their ability to absorb minor shocks. They need good elasticity and strong springs to hold the boot and ski firmly on demanding ground, and should not extend laterally too far away from the ski at the heel, thus impeding the action of the edges on steep hard snow.

Serious skiers will chose a quality light slalom ski with good torsional rigidity for holding power on hard pack, and a lively flex for responsive action on the snow. Length requires careful consideration. Shorter skis give an easier carry on the rucksack and an easier kick turn. However, longer skis have more edge to grip a firm surface and better longitudinal stability for long radius turns and deep snow. Despite a potential lack of manoeuvrability, good skiers of average build are unlikely to choose a ski shorter than two metres.

Adjustable poles may seem to be a good idea, but by their nature they have a weak link and the constant changing of length has a detrimental effect. It is better to use a normal pole with rough insulating tape wrapped round the upper shaft to give a grip for walking or traversing uphill.

Technique

Skiing at an advanced level is instinctive and really requires little thought. One feels the snow with the feet, and by experience and intuition the rest of the body reacts naturally to these pressures. In most ski turns the control comes by applying pressure to or adjusting the angle of the ski edges. Edge control is also vital on steep ground, but in a different way. A turn there at the limit on the steepest snow certainly does not require ski/snow contact throughout the turn, in fact quite the opposite. A jump turn must be developed and in such a way that in the narrower Scottish gullies there is no movement across the slope at the completion of the turn. In such a gully, as, say, South Castle on Ben Nevis or East Gully in Coire Bhrochain, there is often also a natural curve to its slope, and a turn of 170° may well be inadequate as it will send the skier crashing into a rock wall at its side. So the skis must be turned at right angles to the direction of travel.

These turns can be practised on an easy-angled slope, concentrating on technique, balance and control. Stand with the skis across the slope, upper body and hips facing downhill. Most of the weight falls naturally on the edged lower ski, with the uphill ski well advanced. Hop upwards by flexing and extending the legs, and turn the skis while in the air through 180°, thus facing the other way. Meanwhile the upper body remains as quiet as possible, facing down the fall line above the turning skis. Any body or hip turn in the direction of turn will cause a loss of edge and control, particularly on firm snow.

To develop these turns on steeper ground, the poles can be introduced. A single pole can be used as a solidly placed pivot downhill from the feet. When using both poles, the downhill pole may be placed slightly behind the fall line from the feet, and the uphill pole just above the tip of the uphill ski. A well timed double pole plant gives an excellent stable initiation into the turn. Solid pole plants are essential, as a pole that sinks or skids during a turn can be embarassing.

A motivated skier will discover the variations in technique for himself until the commitment and reaction to a turn become instinctive. With practice and growing confidence he will be able to link turns on a slope where once he had difficulty in holding a stable stance.

Skiing down the headwall of Coire an Lochain, Cairn Gorm

M. Burrows-Smith

Snow

The quality of snow is all-important. At 50° on cold hard pack with an inch or so of grippage the skier may be happy and relaxed, while on a 30° slope with a glossy icy sheen he may well be wishing for ice axe and crampons. Along with some old wet snows, spring snow on the turn is the most reliable for steep skiing, particularly if it is undisturbed by climbers' footsteps. Cold snows (which have not melted and refrozen) such as powder, soft and hard slab and cold hard pack can all give excellent skiing with varying degrees of difficulty depending on depth and consistency. Needless to say, there is a potential avalanche risk with wind slab. An optimistic, and perhaps foolhardy, concept is that the skier can constantly be test skiing the slope and will always be the creator of the fracture line. He can then use his skill to maintain his position on the slope! Clearly, however, a thorough knowledge of snow and avalanche conditions is required by anyone attempting steep off-piste descents.

Unfortunately for the skier, if not the climber, Scotland's climate can be temperate as well as arctic. Once a melting action, however slight, has occurred, then the skier may have problems. Breakable crusts and ice névé with no surface roughness are perhaps the worst examples, particulary when they are covered with a little light powder and cannot be seen.

When a wind blows into a gully, rime can be produced. This is all right on a small scale as a little surface roughness may be produced. However, when the rime grows larger and is on an icy base, the effect produced is similar to skiing on ball bearings on an ice rink, making it very difficult to hold an edge.

Névé with good surface roughness can be excellent, but totally unforgiving to technical ineptitude. In mild conditions spring snow and wet snow may be at their best, with a few inches of mush on a firm base giving delightful and flattering skiing until the mush gets really deep and sticky. These snows can appear at any time of the year, and should be taken advantage of to the full.

Angles and Cornices

Skiers, like climbers have difficulty in judging the angles of slopes. There is a natural tendency to over-estimate. Scottish snow gullies have a great variety of angles and shapes. They often have short steep sections, but are rarely of sustained steepness. There are exceptions, for example when a typical grade II gully which normally has several short ice pitches becomes well filled with snow, it will form a sustained steep slope.

The following list gives the average angles of some Scottish gullies and ski slopes. The approximate vertical height over which the angle is measured is included. Note that these are average angles, and all these descents contain steeper sections, often considerably so.

Creag an Leth-choin	Lurcher's Gully	12°	240m
Ben Macdui	Allt Clach nan Taillear	20°	610m
Cairn Gorm, Coire Cas	White Lady	21°	210m
Cairn Gorm, Coire na Ciste	West Wall	30°	180m
Cairn Gorm	March Burn	31°	240m
Cairn Gorm, Coire an t-Sneachda	Alladdin's Couloir	37°	180m
Ben Nevis	No 5 Gully	38°	460m
Seana Bhraigh	Press On Gully	45°	300m
Creag Meagaidh	Cinderella	47°	210m
Ben Nevis	Tower Gully	48°	150m
An Teallach	Lord's Gully	50°	370m
Cairn Gorm, Coire an t-Sneachda	Crotched Gully	51°	180m
Cairn Gorm, Loch Avon Basin	Hell's Lum	52°	180m

This is by no means a graded list of some of the descents already accomplished. As already mentioned, snow quality is far more important than the angle of the slope, so one should only attempt the steeper gullies in good conditions. However, one may also be tempted onto easier angled gullies when conditions are not so favourable, and it is then that problems may arise.

Cornices and the scarp slopes underneath them will often provide a trying start to any descent. The skier who has not warmed up and adjusted to his skis is committing himself at the outset on the most serious and vulnerable part of the descent. Cornices can be hopped, cut down, outflanked, abseiled, side-stepped with an axe for aid, or simply left alone. A tour along the summit rim of Ben Nevis can present a depressing series of dripping monsters. However, there is always the possibility of finding a descent with relatively reasonable access where a cornice may already have collapsed. Roping down over a cornice or side-stepping with an axe down a steep headwall may be tedious, but it may be worthwhile if there is a fine run to be had further down.

Climbing up the gully first is a sensible precaution, particularly when unsure of the conditions. One can stop the ascent at any time when they gully's 'skiability' looks unlikely and start the descent from there. However, this removes a certain sense of adventure, and would be impracticable when attempting to link a number of gullies in an extended ski tour. There is nothing more exciting than seeing a steep gully for the first time from the top and skiing it on sight, hopefully with good control and style.

Where to go

Any grade I gully with reasonable width and good snow cover is a possible descent. Known descents of such routes have been recorded in Scottish Mountaineering Club Journals. They include a surprising variety of mountain areas — Glen Coe, Ben Nevis, Creag Meagaidh, Cairn Gorm, Braeriach, Lochnagar, the Fannaichs, An Teallach, Beinn Dearg and Seana Bhraigh.

Clearly, once technique, nerve and confidence have been developed, the motivated ski mountaineer has magnificent opportunities for exciting adventure in the Scottish mountains.

SCOTTISH MOUNTAINEERING CLUB GUIDEBOOKS AND OTHER PUBLICATIONS

published by the Scottish Mountaineering Trust

DISTRICT GUIDEBOOKS

SOUTHERN UPLANDS	K.M. Andrew and A.A. Thrippleton
SOUTHERN HIGHLANDS	D.J. Bennet
CENTRAL HIGHLANDS	P. Hodgkiss
CAIRNGORMS	A. Watson
WESTERN HIGHLANDS	D.J. Bennet
NORTHERN HIGHLANDS	T. Strang
ISLAND OF SKYE	M. Slesser

GENERAL GUIDEBOOKS

SCOTLAND'S MOUNTAINS	W.H. Murray
THE MUNROS	D.J. Bennet (Editor)
MUNRO'S TABLES	J.C. Donaldson (Editor)

SCRAMBLERS' GUIDE

BLACK CUILLIN RIDGE	S.P. Bull

CLIMBERS' GUIDEBOOKS

SELECTIVE ROCK AND ICE GUIDES

GLEN COE AND GLEN ETIVE	K.V. Crocket
LOCHABER AND BADENOCH	A.C. Stead and J.R. Marshall
SKYE	J.R. Mackenzie

COMPREHENSIVE GUIDES

THE CAIRNGORMS	A. Fyffe and A. Nisbet
BEN NEVIS	J.R. Marshall
ARRAN	W.M.M. Wallace and W. Skidmore
NORTH EAST OUTCROPS	D. Dinwoodie (Editor)
CREAG DUBH AND CREAG A BARNS	D. Cuthbertson
CENTRAL AND SOUTHERN SCOTLAND	J. Handren (Editor)

MAPS

THE BLACK CUILLIN, ISLAND OF SKYE	J. Renny and A. Kassyk
GLEN COE	J. Renny

OTHER TITLES

BEN NEVIS: BRITAIN'S HIGHEST MOUNTAIN	K.V. Crocket
A CHANCE IN A MILLION. SCOTTISH AVALANCHES	R. Barton and B. Wright

SCOTTISH MOUNTAINEERING CLUB JOURNAL Published annually in June, includes articles and notes of interest and comprehensive information on New Routes in Scotland.

All the above titles available from Cordee, 3a De Montfort Street, Leicester LE1 7HD.